Longman
TESTS IN CONTEXT 3

J·B·Heaton

Longman

INTRODUCTION

This series of three books contains topic-based tests, each test dealing with one common topic or theme. The tests can thus be used in conjunction with specific topics which are taught or which arise from the course work. Alternatively, the tests can be used on their own, thereby forming a topic-based syllabus.

The tests will be found most suitable for use at the following levels:

	English taught as a foreign language	English taught as a second language
Book 1	Elementary level	Lower elementary level
Book 2	Lower intermediate level	Upper elementary level
Book 3	Intermediate level	Lower intermediate level

All the tests consist of objective items, and thus teachers should experience little difficulty in marking the tests and in adopting suitable marking schemes. This also helps to increase the reliability of each test. However, teachers are reminded that they should complement all objective testing by such subjective tests as oral activities and free-writing.

Like all classroom tests, these tests are most useful when they are closely related to the teaching which takes place prior to their use and in follow-up work. Consequently, the tests function best as progress tests for use in the classroom rather than as selection or proficiency tests. The tests can be given regularly (e.g. once every week or fortnight) and can be used to focus students' attention on specific topics and areas of language. Used informally in this way, the tests will serve both to reinforce learning and to motivate students.

Each test uses realia wherever possible, thus constantly reminding students that they are performing real tasks in English and that English is a living language, used as a means of communication in the daily lives of ordinary people. However, the language level of the students using the book has been taken into account at all times and an attempt has been made to avoid cultural bias as much as possible. For learners of English living in Britain and in countries where English is used as a first or second language, the use of realia reflects those tasks which students will be called upon to perform in real life. In all cases, the tests will make the learning of English seem more relevant to students.

All the tests have been carefully graded, following both a structural and a functional/notional syllabus. Moreover, since the tests highlight important and useful topic areas, they can be used to supplement any syllabus, whether the syllabus is based on topics, functions or grammar.

Each book contains a brief guide for teachers, indicating suitable preparation and teaching for each test. However, it must be emphasised that the books are also useful for work on a self-access basis by students learning English on their own. Answers to all the test questions are given in a detachable key included in the book. Furthermore, there are blanks in the marking scheme for entering the student's score for each question. In this way students can follow their progress as they work through the tests.

FOR THE TEACHER

TEST 1

Theme   Education
Grammar   Connectives: *because, because of, for, as*
Gerund and infinitive forms
Functions   Giving reasons, information and advice, complaining
Vocabulary   *lesson, timetable, syllabus, curriculum, subject, course, teach, lecture, instruct, describe, demonstrate, explain*
Realia   School report, articles

Teaching guide

1 Put on the board an imaginary school/college report showing the marks which a student has obtained but *not* the comments. Discuss the marks with the class and write short comments on the board against each mark.

2 Pair work: short dialogues in which students talk about their own school progress reports. (This will be helped by students bringing their previous reports to class with them.)

3 Ask students about their plans to go to university or college and talk briefly about some of the subjects offered there.

4 Try to get hold of an advertisement (or preferably a brochure) containing information about English courses in a particular school or institute. Read extracts aloud and discuss the course with the class.

5 Writing consolidation to be given after Question 5: working in small groups, students should be instructed to write a short letter applying for a holiday English course in Britain (or any other suitable country). Note: each group should write one letter.

6 Working in groups (and helped as far as possible by the teacher), students should be encouraged to discuss the subject of homework in preparation for Question 6. Two or three simple questions might be given to stimulate discussion, e.g. *Should students be given homework? If so, for how long each evening? If not, what could replace homework? Should students be allowed to seek help from one another or from their parents when doing homework? Why (not)?*

TEST 2

Theme   Processes
Grammar   Verbs: Passive without agent
Functions   Describing processes and giving instructions
Vocabulary   *process, step, stage, manufacture, transport, result, description, first, afterwards, in turn, eventually, finally*
Realia   Cooking instructions, scientific and technical articles

Teaching guide

1 Introductory activity: bring a camera to the lesson and ask a student to show you how to load a film in it. Write each step on the board as the student explains (using the active voice). Then let one or two other students explain, looking at the board (as a prompt) where necessary. Finally, go through the steps once again, changing the active into the passive voice.

2 Ask students what happens to letters when they are posted. Draw the various steps on the board, using simple line drawings of envelopes, letterboxes, bags, vans, etc.

3 Group work: students should explain to one another how to cook rice. Each group should then write a short paragraph about cooking rice. Compare the finished results, putting one paragraph on the board (written in the active) and another on the board (written in the passive) if at all possible. If all the paragraphs have been written in the active voice, write only one paragraph on the board, later changing the verbs into the passive where possible.

4 Introduce the appropriate vocabulary for describing the different steps/stages in a process, including such adverbs as *firstly, afterwards, in turn*, etc.

5 Try to obtain an illustration of the food cycle (often shown in one picture in textbooks and junior encyclopaedias). Working in groups, students describe to one another the food cycle. If it is not possible to obtain pictures for the food cycle, use pictures for any other natural cycle (e.g. the rain cycle).

TEST 3

Theme   The environment
Grammar   *so* + adj .... *to; so* + adj .... *that; too* + adj .... *to; enough* + noun; adj + *enough*
Functions   Talking about the future, predicting; talking about quantity and amount
Vocabulary   *pollution, environment, atmosphere, resource, problem, effect, population, wildlife, wasteland, protect, transform*
Realia   Notice, letter, articles

Teaching guide

1 Introduction: ask the class what they think is the most precious thing human beings have. Show a few pictures of the countryside throughout the world and talk about the environment. Why is it so precious? How is it being destroyed? What is man doing to preserve it?

2 Group or pair work: students talk about a problem in their area, e.g. the increasing amount of traffic in their town or city. The group (or pair) then write a letter about this problem to their local newspaper.

3 In what ways are modern industrial developments harmful? Working in groups, students discuss this problem and ways of helping to solve it.

4 Show students pictures of an Egyptian sphinx. After describing it, students should discuss ways in which they think it is being damaged by modern civilisation. They should then proceed to read the paragraphs in Question 5 (unless all the questions in this test are being attempted at the same time).

5 If possible, show photographs of smoke coming from factory chimneys, gases from car exhausts, etc. (i.e. illustrating the pollution of the atmosphere) in preparation for Question 6.

TEST 4

Theme	Humour
Grammar	Connectives: *should, ought to* Interrogative pronouns
Functions	Telling jokes, identifying misprints, describing humour
Vocabulary	*joke, practical joke, humour, comedy, cartoon, riddle, burst out (laughing), funny, witty, amusing*
Realia	Jokes, letters, newspaper extracts

Teaching guide

1 Introduction: tell the class one or two jokes in English before asking individual students to come out and tell their favourite joke in English. How hard is it to tell a joke in another language? Are there any differences between humour in your country and English humour?

2 Read aloud (for listening comprehension) the short story in Question 1 and ask questions based on it. Ask students what the doctor ought/oughtn't to have done and what the woman should/shouldn't have done.

3 Revise or teach important vocabulary connected with humour, using a newspaper (for *cartoons*, etc.), a television/radio programme guide (for

comedies). Give one or two examples of *practical jokes*, etc. Tell the class one or two riddles, first in the mother tongue and then in English. Revise the following synonyms: *funny, witty, amusing, humorous*.

4 Group work: students bring their own joke books, etc. and use them to tell their favourite jokes in English. The best joke in each group could be written down (in English).

5 Show the class examples of amusing misprints from newspapers, e.g. *dish* for *fish*, etc. Which misprints are funny and which are not? Why?

6 After this test has been completed by students, go over any difficult points, etc., showing students why certain jokes or stories are amusing (avoiding lengthy explanations as far as possible).

TEST 5

Theme	Astrology
Grammar	Verbs: Future simple tense
Functions	Making predictions, giving advice
Vocabulary	*astrology, horoscope, birthday, birth sign, prediction, influence, opportunity, change, career, romance, travel*
Realia	Predictions from newspapers, letters

Teaching guide

1 Introduction: bring to the class one or two magazines on astrology or cut out the relevant sections from a newspaper (if newspapers in your country contain such sections). Introduce the topic by reading aloud the predictions for a few students in the class, first asking which students were born on certain dates.

2 Introduce the vocabulary listed in this section and mention also a) the names of the star signs, e.g. Capricorn, Aquarius, Aries, Cancer, Leo, Libra, etc. and b) the names of some important planets in astrology, e.g. Mars, Venus, Saturn, Uranus. However, do not attempt to teach the positions of the planets in the sky, etc.

3 Pair work: let students practise using the future simple tense to talk about their future plans and intentions.

4 Pair work: one student should pretend to be an astrologer and the other student should give his/her date of birth and ask what he/she will do in the future. Later, these roles should be reversed.

5 Group work: tell the class your date of birth and write a short letter on the board, asking an astrologer about your future. Working in small groups, students should adopt the role of astrologers and write (group) replies.

TEST 6

Theme Air travel
Grammar Determiners: *each, every, all, other another*
Functions Giving advice, describing a process, classifying
Vocabulary *aircraft, terminal, arrival, immigration, passport, handbaggage, Customs, (customs) duty, trolley, declare, claim*
Realia Airline leaflets, timetable, etc., aircraft recognition extract

Teaching guide

1 Revise articles and determiners (*a, some, any, much, many*) with countable and uncountable nouns connected with aeroplanes and air travel.
2 Put on the board a simplified version of an airline timetable, showing flight numbers, destinations, departure times, etc. Go through this timetable with the class, asking simple questions concerning departure times, etc.
3 Pair work: if possible, give out actual airline timetables to one student in each pair and give the name of a place (i.e. the destination) on a piece of paper to the other student in the pair. The former student should pretend to be a travel agent, and the latter should pretend to be planning to travel by air to the destination written on the paper. Each pair of students should then act out the roles assigned to them.
4 Teach the vocabulary connected with air travel and airport terminals (including *customs* and *immigration*).
5 Show the class an air ticket if possible. Look at the reading text in Question 5 and briefly describe to the class the various steps involved in booking a flight.
6 Finally, show an illustration of a particular aircraft and talk briefly about it. Then instruct students to work in pairs. Give one student in each pair a picture of a commercial plane and tell the other student to ask questions about the plane, e.g. its length, the wing span, the number of passengers it can carry, its cruising speed, etc. The other student should attempt to answer these questions from the information in the picture. If this information is not shown, he/she should make up the answers to the questions.

TEST 7

Theme Surveys
Grammar Reported speech
Functions Reporting what others have said, understanding information in surveys
Vocabulary *(opinion) poll, survey, population, cross-section, balance, sample, finding, prediction, forecast, opinion, view, conduct, carry out, reflect, represent, select*
Realia Surveys and simple statistics

Teaching guide

1 Introduce the vocabulary related to opinion polls and surveys. Refer to one or two recent surveys which have been carried out in your country. Talk about these surveys and then get students to think about how the surveys were actually carried out.
2 Group work: show students how to conduct an opinion poll, instructing them to work in small groups. Each group decides on six to ten questions to ask the other students in the class to find out their views concerning a topical matter, e.g. the place of pop music in society, English food, modern technology, tourism, morals and behaviour in modern society, etc. After this activity has been completed, the groups report their findings. Put these findings on the board in what you consider to be the most suitable form, e.g. a table, a graph.
3 Writing: students should write a short paragraph giving the information contained in one of the tables or graphs on the board.
4 Consolidation: students should write a short report giving the information contained in the table in Question 5 after they have completed this test paper.
5 Project: with older, more advanced students it is possible to design a project involving going outside the school/college and interviewing the public. Under your guidance, the class should first decide on a few suitable topics, e.g. people's attitudes to living abroad, using English as an international language, what older people think about modern youth, etc. The class should then work out appropriate questions to ask. Reports from groups of students should be given to the whole class after the interviews have been conducted. Finally, group reports should be prepared, using all the information obtained and containing tables or graphs where helpful.

TEST 8

Theme Revision
Grammar Revision of verbs, connectives, etc.
Functions Giving and obtaining information, making predictions, describing processes

Vocabulary	Revision of vocabulary concerned with humour and astrology
Realia	Book and newspaper extracts

Teaching guide

1 Show several travel brochures and ask students questions about the places. Many students will not be able to answer questions about the climate of the places, the sights to see, and the best way of reaching these places. Tell the class that in a recent survey in Britain it was found that many travel agents had difficulty when asked similar questions.

2 Ask students what they think planes and air travel will be like in fifty years. Use this activity as a way of practising the future simple tense (in preparation for Question 2).

3 Pair work: give one student in each pair some pictures showing a particular process. The student with the pictures briefly describes the process and his/her partner must then guess what is being carried out, manufactured, grown, etc. The pictures can then be collected by the teacher and re-distributed to the class, the other student in each pair describing the process this time. This will provide the necessary preparation/revision for Question 5 in this test.

4 Lead a class discussion on what constitutes the best size for English classes in order to introduce the subject of the reading extract in Question 6.

TEST 9

Theme	Computers
Grammar	*like, as, so, such, although, because,* etc.
Functions	Classifying, narrating past events and developments, describing and comparing
Vocabulary	*computer, screen, function (keys), socket, monitor, disk, disk drive, printer, joystick, programme*
Realia	Book extracts, buying guide (survey)

Teaching guide

1 Introduction: talk about computers, bringing a home computer to the class if possible. Mention the various programming languages, but don't attempt to explain them at any length.

2 Put on the board a typical (short) computer programme, pointing out significant features to the class.

3 Teach the vocabulary necessary, using either a computer itself or a large picture of a computer.

4 Pair work: give one student in each pair details of

a certain computer and the other student in the pair details of another computer. Encourage the students to ask and answer questions about their computers and to make helpful comparisons. Both students should later write a joint report, comparing their two computers.

5 Role-play: working in groups, students can be encouraged to act out roles. One student in the group should be given a catalogue containing information about several computers (with very different features), while the other students in the group should be assigned different roles and be instructed to buy computers for different purposes, e.g. one student might want a small computer on which to play games, another might want a home computer to write programmes or to work through certain educational programmes, another student might be a businessman who wants a computer for a small office, another student might want several computers for a large company, etc.

TEST 10

Theme	Disasters
Grammar	Verbs: Past continuous tense; *while* clauses
Functions	Describing disasters, reporting past events
Vocabulary	*fire, typhoon, earthquake, tidal wave, plague, volcano, drought, tornado, landslide, flood, famine*
Realia	Newspaper extracts, letter, advertisement leaflet

Teaching guide

1 Bring to the class a recent newspaper (if possible, a newspaper published on the same day as the lesson) and read out one or two reports of disasters. Ask the class why disasters and bad news are reported and good news largely ignored.

2 Describe a tornado and the damage it can do, showing photographs if possible.

3 Pair work: one student should pretend to have witnessed a disaster, e.g. an earthquake, a landslide, a tornado and another pupil should interview him/her. Later, a short article can be written by both students about the disaster.

4 Discussion: ask students if they know of any organisation which helps people in time of disaster. How useful are these organisations? What can be done to make sure that help reaches the right people (i.e. the victims of the disaster)?

5 Group work: students should 'invent' an organisation which can help disaster victims. The

group should then write a poster or an extract for the cover of a brochure, briefly describing the organisation, its aims and the work it does. The aim of the poster or brochure is to persuade people to give money to the organisation.

TEST 11

Theme	Inventions
Grammar	Verbs: Passive with agent
Functions	Reporting and describing inventions
Vocabulary	*invention, manufacture, laboratory, experiment, test, patent, device, ingenious, practical, original, revolutionary, design*
Realia	Newspaper report, book extract and diagram

Teaching guide

1   As Question 1 takes the form of a new test item type, it will be useful to give students practice in doing this type of item. Simply take a short paragraph from a book (if possible, on the subject of inventions or on a particular invention) and introduce one grammatical error into each sentence. Divide each sentence into four parts, labelled A, B, C and D, and instruct students to find the part of the sentence containing an error.

2   Using the information in Question 1, talk about the history of printing and show (if possible) pictures of early printing machines.

3   Introduce some of the vocabulary related to inventions, e.g. *device, patent, design, ingenious, original, revolutionary.* Teach this vocabulary in context as far as possible.

4   Group work: encourage students in groups to 'invent' something and to draw their invention (giving them ideas if necessary). Each group should then write a short description of its invention and the purposes for which it can be used. Later, the groups will draw their inventions on the board and read aloud their descriptions to the class.

TEST 12

Theme	Habits and customs
Grammar	Verbs: *used to*; Past simple tense
Functions	Talking about past habits and customs, describing and classifying
Vocabulary	*custom, tradition, practice, habit, routine, festival, usually, invariably, regularly, customarily, habitually, frequently*
Realia	Book extracts

Teaching guide

1   Introduce the topic by talking a little about some of the changes which you have seen in your own lifetime, e.g. the spread of television, the increase in the number of cars on the roads, etc. Encourage students to comment on changes in lifestyle, habits and customs, etc. since they were small children.

2   Introduce the topic of Atlantis, describing the legendary island and civilisation (and the subsequent searches for this island). Arouse students' interest in the mystery surrounding Atlantis (see Question 2).

3   Teach the appropriate vocabulary concerned with habits and customs (especially such adverbs as *traditionally, usually, invariably, customarily, habitually, consistently,* etc.)

4   Group work: copy the line drawings of the various hats in Question 5 and give each group copies of the drawings. Instruct students to describe the various hats, first orally and then in (group) writing.

5   Talk a little about Ancient Mexico and the Aztecs in order to stimulate interest in the subject of the reading text in Question 6. If there is a school/college library, encourage students to find out for themselves about Ancient Mexico from books or reference works written either in English or in their mother tongue.

TEST 13

Theme	Commerce and Industry
Grammar	Verbs: Past perfect tense
Functions	Reporting, presenting information verbally and in visual form
Vocabulary	*personnel, finance, public relations, sales, supply, demand, coordinate, stand (at), level off, fluctuate, peak, average*
Realia	Newspaper article, sales reports, graphs

Teaching guide

1   Introduce the topic of Question 1 by telling or reading a success story in business (i.e. 'from rags to riches').

2   Group work: give out newspaper articles or extracts containing success stories (preferably in English – but, if not possible, in the students' mother tongue) and encourage students to discuss in groups the reasons for the success (or failure). What qualities should a successful business person have?

3   Introduce in context some of the vocabulary

required for describing business organisations and developments.

4 Describe briefy the increase in sales, levelling off and fall in sales of a certain product over two or three years. Draw a simple graph (see Page 51) on the board and then get students to describe the sales pattern from the graph.

5 Before students attempt Question 6, make sure they understand the words *fluctuate* and *marked/dramatic rise/fall*.

TEST 14

Theme	Energy
Grammar	*If-clauses* (Type 2): *would .... + if + past simple tense*
Functions	Hypothesising, talking about possible developments and results
Vocabulary	*source, supply, reserve, resource, power, fossil fuel, exhaust, renew, renewable, alternative, consumption*
Realia	Book extracts, newspaper articles

Teaching guide

1 Introduction: talk briefly about the ways in which energy affects your life and that of your students. How do most people cook in your area? Do they use wood, charcoal, gas or electricity? If there are cool times of the year, how do people keep warm? What do cars and buses run on? From where is this fuel obtained?

2 Write on the board a list of the main forms of energy. Don't forget about solar energy, wind energy and hydropower.

3 Teach or revise the first two types of *if*-clauses, i.e. a) future simple tense + *if* + present simple tense and b) *would* + *if* + past simple tense. Make statements about energy supplies and ask questions using these structures, e.g. *What will happen if the price of oil goes up? What do you think will happen if we use up all the world's oil supplies? What would you do if there was an electricity breakdown? What do you think would happen if there was a big explosion at a nuclear energy plant?*

4 Introduce the vocabulary related to all the various chief forms of energy.

5 Working in small groups, students should make a list of all the various forms of energy and write one or two sentences describing the chief advantages and disadvantages of each energy form, e.g. *Solar energy will not run out and will not pollute the atmosphere. However, it is difficult to obtain energy from the sun in many parts of the world and the equipment needed costs a lot of money.*

TEST 15

Theme	Accidents
Grammar	Verbs: Past perfect tense
	If-clauses (Type 3): *would have .... + if + past perfect tense*
Functions	Talking about accidents, understanding accident reports and graphs
Vocabulary	*accident, bystander, witness, first–aid, emergency (department), shock, wreck, wreckage, injure, insure, compensation*
Realia	Accident reports, graph

Teaching guide

1 Use a photograph or drawing to talk about an accident. Give a simple verbal report of what happened, using the past simple and past perfect tenses.

2 Pair work: give students a picture of a road accident and get them to participate in a simple role-play. Both students pretend to have been involved in the accident and refuse to admit responsibility for the accident. Each blames the other.

3 Introduce in a variety of contexts the vocabulary related to accidents.

4 Group work: draw on the board the scene of an accident (or show a picture to the class) but do not give a detailed account of it. Let each group guess what has happened and say who was responsible for the accident. After discussing the accident, each group should then write an accident report. On completion of this activity, the reports should be read to the class.

TEST 16

Theme	Revision
Grammar	Verbs: Tenses; passive voice, etc.
Functions	Talking about past events, disasters and accidents, describing present activities and developments, and classifying
Vocabulary	Revision of vocabulary concerned with alternative medicine and computers
Realia	Newspaper reports, book extracts

Teaching guide

1 Listening comprehension: talk about a recent disaster/accident and read aloud the newspaper report about the disaster/accident. Ask questions about the report.

2 Draw a simple graph on the board, showing (imaginary) increases, fluctuations, etc. in the sales of cars in your country. Instruct students to work in groups and produce group written reports of the sales. Each report should end by predicting

future sales (based on the latest trends shown in the graph).

3   Bring along a drawing of your latest invention – preferably humorous, e.g. your latest automatic marking machine, a device to help drivers to pass other cars when the road is too narrow to overtake, a robot which can help to clean your house, etc! Working in pairs or small groups, students should discuss how your invention works and then write a short paragraph describing it. Let most of the pairs or groups read aloud their descriptions.

4   Talk briefly about sources of energy and introduce the following words and phrases: *fossils, geothermal, hydro-power, renewable, non-polluting, practicable, earth's heat load.*

EDUCATION

1 GRAMMAR RECOGNITION (10 marks)

Read the following school progress report. Put a circle round the letter of the correct word or words to use in each blank.

Subject reports		
Science	30%	Has not done very well this term [1] ___ several absences from school.
Maths	15%	Has scored low marks in the examination [2] ___ he has not done much homework.
History	42%	[3] ___ his failure to answer the last two questions, his examination result was very disappointing.
Geography	50%	Fair, but can do better [4] ___ he tries harder. Has missed a lot of homework.
Social Studies	53%	[5] ___ he has made a lot of progress, he still needs to try harder and do more work, especially at home.
English	49%	He can speak fairly fluently [6] ___ his written work is poor.
Art	82%	An excellent result. He always works hard [7] ___ he is very keen on painting.
Sport	—	Has improved a lot [8] ___ he is now much taller and stronger.

Class teacher's report

His examination results are not very good [9] ___ he does not seem to try very hard. He works hard for a short time [10] ___ he finds it difficult to concentrate for longer periods. However, he is a popular member of the class [11] ___ his cheerfulness and willingness to help both the teacher and his classmates.

1 A as   B as of   C because   (D) because of
2 A because   B but   C after   D if
3 A For   B Because of   C As for   D By
4 A if   B because   C or   D and
5 A But   B Although   C As   D After
6 A and   B but   C because   D when
7 A but   B as   C or   D although
8 A when   B before   C because   D if
9 A if   B but   C before   D as
10 A before   B if   C but   D or
11 A because of   B as for   C and   D as

2 GRAMMAR PRODUCTION (10 marks)

Read the following conversation and then make suitable changes to it, using the verbs in bold type. Write your answers in the blanks.

A Do you enjoy (¹**be**) _____ *being* _____ at university?

B Yes, I do, although I often miss (²**see**) _____ my old school friends.

A Don't you mind (³**travel**) _____ so far every day?

B No, it only takes me an hour or so (⁴**get**) _____ there. Sometimes I manage
   (⁵**work**) _____ on the bus.

A Don't you find all the noise and people prevent you from (⁶**concentrate**) _____?

B Not really. I usually do a bit of reading. Are you still at school or have you got a job?

A I'm still at school. I hope (⁷**go**) _____ to university next year, but I haven't applied
   anywhere yet.

B I suggest you (⁸**apply**) _____ soon – its' getting late.

A Where would you advise me (⁹**apply**) _____ ?

B What subjects are you studying?

A Physics, chemistry and biology. I want (¹⁰**study**) _____ physics at university.

B I would recommend (¹¹**apply**) _____ to Newton University first of all, but why
   don't you apply to one or two other universities as well?

3 VOCABULARY (5 marks)

Put a circle round the letter of the correct word to use in each blank.

1 LINDA What's the next _____ ?
          (A) lesson   B timetable   C programme   D hour

2 DAVID Just a moment. Let me look at my _____ .
          A timetable   B class   C syllabus   D plan

3 LINDA Oh, it's history – my favourite _____ .
          A knowledge   B study   C subject   D matter

4 DAVID I usually like history, but I didn't care for the _____ last year. We did nineteenth century
          European history. It was boring!
          A syllabus   B study   C plan   D timetable

5 LINDA We're studying the Roman Empire this year, and I'm also taking a _____ in archaeology at
          evening school.
          A lesson   B course   C syllabus   D curriculum

6 DAVID It's a pity that archaeology isn't included in the _____ here.
          A lesson   B period   C curriculum   D topic

4 VOCABULARY (5 marks)

Read the following sentences and write the correct word in each blank. Choose the words from the list below.

describes   shows   learns   explains   teaches   lectures

Mr Shaw [1] _**teaches**_ physics at the University of Hong Kong and [2]_____ mostly to third-year students. The students like him a lot because he [3]_____ how things work in simple language. Mr Shaw says that he often [4]_____ a lot from his students. His wife is an English teacher in a secondary school. In her lessons she [5]_____ her pupils how to write short stories and [6]_____ people and scenes she knows in her stories.

5 READING (10 marks)

Read the following article about holiday English Language courses in Scotland. Write the correct word in each blank.

Holiday courses in Scotland

Our classes take place for three hours every morning from Monday to Friday. The maximum class size is twelve and the average is ten. We use modern methods of [1] _**teaching**_ and learning, and the school has a language laboratory, a video camera and recorder. You will only be successful in improving your English, however, if you work hard and [2]_____ speaking English as much as you can. You will take a short [3]_____ in English as soon as you arrive. In this way, we can put you in a [4]_____ at the most suitable level.

There are two classes at the Elementary level; one is for complete [5]_____ and the other is for students who know only a little English. In both classes you will practise simple conversations.

In the class at the Intermediate level you will have a lot of [6]_____ in communicating in real-life situations because we help you to *use* the English you have previously [7]_____ in your own country. You will also have the chance to improve your [8]_____ of English grammar and to build up your vocabulary.

The emphasis is on oral communication practice in a wide variety of situations at the advanced [9]_____ . You will learn how to use language correctly and appropriately when you [10]_____ to native speakers. In addition, you will develop such study skills as reading efficiently, writing articles and reports, and note-taking from books and [11]_____ .

6 READING (10 marks)

Read the following passage. Write true (T) or false (F) for each of the sentences below, according to the information given. If the information is not given, put a question mark (?).

Many people now think that teachers give pupils too much homework. They say that it is unnecessary for children to work at home in their free time. Moreover, they argue that most teachers do not properly plan the homework tasks they give to pupils. The result is that pupils have to repeat tasks which they have already done at school.

Recently in Greece many parents complained about the difficult homework which teachers gave to their children. The parents said that most of the homework was a waste of time, and they wanted to stop it. Spain and Turkey are two countries which stopped homework recently. In Denmark, West Germany and several other countries in Europe, teachers cannot set homework at weekends. In Holland, teachers allow pupils to stay at school to do their homework. The children are free to help one another. Similar arrangements also exist in some British schools.

Most people agree that homework is unfair. A pupil who can do his homework in a quiet and comfortable room is in a much better position than a pupil who does his homework in a small, noisy room with the television on. Some parents help their children with their homework. Other parents take no interest at all in their children's homework.

It is important, however, that teachers talk to parents about homework. A teacher should suggest suitable tasks for parents to do with their children. Parents are often better at teaching their own children!

1 T According to the writer, many parents would like their children to have less homework.

2 ☐ Many teachers think that pupils should have homework.

3 ☐ Parents think that pupils shouldn't have to do a lot of work in their leisure time at home.

4 ☐ A lot of homework has not been planned properly, according to many parents.

5 ☐ Parents say that most teachers give homework which is different from the work the pupils have done in class.

6 ☐ Greek parents thought their children's homework was too easy.

7 ☐ Children do not have any homework now in Turkey.

8 ☐ In some countries in Europe teachers are allowed to give children homework only at weekends.

9 ☐ Children can do their homework at school and help one another in some schools in Britain.

10 ☐ Only a small number of people think that homework is fair.

11 ☐ Teachers should advise parents about how to work together with their children at home.

TEST 2

PROCESSES

1 GRAMMAR RECOGNITION (10 marks)

Read the following conversation between a shop assistant and someone who is buying a camera. Put a circle round the letter of the correct word to use in each blank.

LEILA   How ^{1}____ this camera?
          A load do I   B I load   C I do load   (D) do I load

ASSISTANT   Well, can you ^{2}____ this black button here?
              A see   B saw   C seen   D seeing

              If ^{3}____ , the back cover opens.
              A it pulls up   B it's pulled up   C it's pulling up   D it pull up

ASSISTANT   The button ^{4}____the back cover. Now the camera is open.
              A is unlocked   B is unlocking   C unlocks   D is being unlocked

LEILA ^{5}____ the film in the camera now?
          A I do put   B Am I putting   C Do I put   D I'm putting

ASSISTANT   Yes, first ^{6}____ the film out of the small can.
              A takes   B is taking   C is taken   D take

              Make sure this part of the film ^{7}____ upwards – like this.
              A facing   B to face   C faced   D faces

LEILA   What happens if I ^{8}____ it in the other way round?
          A put   B puts   C putting   D not put

ASSISTANT   Well, it ^{9}____ if it's the wrong way.
              A won't fit   B not fit   C it isn't fitting   D isn't fitted

LEILA   What do I do now?

ASSISTANT   Now put the end of it in the spool here and wind the film on. Turn this handle and then press the red button. Now close the cover of the camera. The film must then be ^{10}____ on once again.
              A winds   B winding   C wound   D wind

LEILA   The number '1' ^{11}____ in the window, and I'm ready to take my first picture!
          A appears   B appearing   C appear   D is appeared

2 GRAMMAR PRODUCTION (5 marks)

Read the following paragraph and then put any suitable verb from the list below in each blank. Write each verb in its correct form.

| deliver   sort   take   send   collect   stamp |

The letters [1] _**are collected**_ from the post box. Then a postman [2]_____

them to the post office. At the post office, they [3]_____ by a machine so that the

stamps cannot be used again. Next they [4]_____ carefully and put into bags before

[5]_____ to other post offices for further sorting. Finally, a postman

[6]_____ the letters to the addresses shown on the envelopes.

3 GRAMMAR PRODUCTION (5 marks)

Study the pictures. Then complete each sentence describing the whole process of cooking rice.

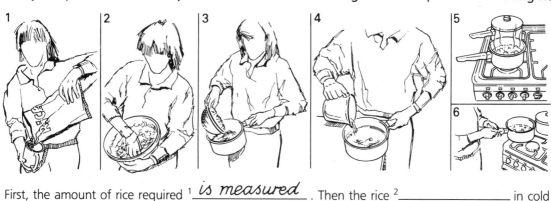

First, the amount of rice required [1] _**is measured**_ . Then the rice [2]_____ in cold

water. When it is clean, the rice [3]_____ in a pan. Next the rice [4]_____

with water. The rice [5]_____ slowly for twenty minutes. Finally, the pan

[6]_____ off the stove.

4 VOCABULARY (5 marks)

Write the correct word in each blank. A dash (–) is shown for each missing letter and some letters are given in each word.

The following is a [1]d _e_ scr _i_ pt _i o_ n of the food cycle. [2]F _____ t, small birds and animals eat

insects. [3]A __t __ w__ds, many of these small birds and animals are in [4]t__n eaten by

larger birds and animals. All animals, birds and insects [5]ev__t____ly die, and their bodies

decay. [6]F__n____ly, the dead matter is absorbed by plants and trees.

5 VOCABULARY (5 marks)

Read the following paragraph. Put a circle round the letter of the correct word to use in each blank.

The first ¹____ in the ²____ of paper is to cut down suitable trees and chop them up. The pieces of wood are then ³____ to a paper mill. In the next ⁴____ of the ⁵____ , the pieces of wood are ground up and mixed with water. The ⁶____ is wood pulp.

1 **A** foot **(B)** step **C** yard **D** walk
2 **A** industry **B** creation **C** product **D** manufacture
3 **A** transmitted **B** transformed **C** transported **D** translated
4 **A** stage **B** platform **C** act **D** event
5 **A** produce **B** process **C** problem **D** programme
6 **A** product **B** cause **C** condition **D** finish

6 READING (5 marks)

Use the diagrams to help you to put these sentences in order. They describe how a boat can use a lock to move to a higher part of the canal. Write 1–6 in the correct boxes.

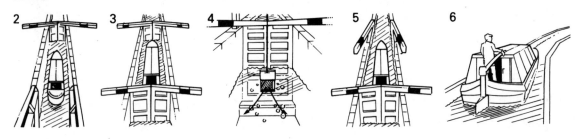

A ☐ The boat can then proceed up the canal.

B ☐ Water is run into the lock from the upper level through small holes in the gate.

C ☐ When a boat has to be raised to a higher level, it enters the lock with the upper gates shut.

D ☐ When the level has reached that of the upper part of the canal, the upper gates are fully opened.

E [1] A lock is a way of raising or lowering boats at a point where the water on a canal is at a different level.

F ☐ Once the boat is in the lock, the lower gates are then closed.

7 READING (5 marks)

Read the following sentences about the way sound is produced in the human body.
Put all the sentences in order. Write 1–7 in the correct boxes.

A ☐ The air which pushes through the narrow slit then makes the vocal cords vibrate.

B [1] Your voice box is at the top of your windpipe.

C ☐ When you are not talking, this slit is always wide open and the air passes through it without making a noise.

D ☐ The sounds of your voice are produced in this way.

E ☐ When you talk, the vocal cords become tight and make the slit narrower.

F [4] On both sides of the slit there are flaps which are your vocal cords.

G ☐ In the middle of your voice box there is a narrow opening, or slit, like a letterbox.

8 READING (10 marks)

Read the passage below about how sugar is produced. Write the correct word
in each blank.

Sugar

Sugar cane is grown in hot countries like Cuba and the West Indies, where there is a heavy

rainfall. At harvest time the cane is cut as close to the ground as possible in order to keep all the juice,

or sap, in each long stalk.

The ^{1}___cane___ is then taken to a mill, where it is cut into a lot of small pieces.

^{2}_____ the sap is squeezed out by heavy rollers. The sap is cleaned and then boiled until

crystals appear. It is necessary, however, to separate these brown ^{3}_____ from the sap. This is

^{4}_____ by putting the mixture into a huge machine containing a drum which

^{5}_____ at high speed. The ^{6}_____ spins out of the machine, leaving the crystals

behind.

The brown crystals are raw ^{7}_____ . This sugar is loaded onto large ships and

^{8}_____ to other countries, where it is refined and packaged before being sent to shops.

The sap which remains after the raw sugar has been ^{9}_____ is called 'molasses' and is

used to ^{10}_____ rum and yeast. ^{11}_____ is wasted; even the tops of the canes are

used for making cattle food.

TEST 3

THE ENVIRONMENT

1 GRAMMAR RECOGNITION (10 marks)

Read the following passage. Put the correct word from the list below in each blank. You may use some words more than once.

| so   so much   so many   too   too much   too many   enough |

Save the Earth!

We are all slowly destroying the earth. The seas and rivers are ¹___**too**___ dirty to swim in. There is ²_____ smoke in the air that it is unhealthy to live in many of the world's cities. In one well-known city, for example, poisonous gases from cars pollute the air ³_____ that traffic policemen have to wear oxygen masks.

We have cut down ⁴_____ trees that there are now vast areas of wasteland all over the world. As a result, farmers in parts of Africa cannot grow ⁵_____ to eat. In certain countries in Asia there is ⁶_____ little rice. Moreover, we do not take ⁷_____ care of the countryside. Wild animals are quickly disappearing. For instance, tigers are rare in India now because we have killed ⁸_____ for them to survive. However, it isn't ⁹_____ simply to talk about the problem. We must act now before it is ¹⁰_____ late to do anything about it. Join us now. Save the Earth. This is ¹¹_____ important to ignore.

2 GRAMMAR PRODUCTION (5 marks)

Read the following letter and write one word or more in each blank.

Dear Sir,
There are now ¹ _so_ many cars in the centre of Newtown ²_____ it is becoming impossible to park. There are no large car parks at all and there aren't ³_____ parking spaces on the streets. It is also getting ⁴_____ dangerous for people to do their shopping in the city centre. The situation is ⁵_____ bad that many people are beginning to go shopping in Dartford and Redfern. The streets in the centre of Newtown aren't wide ⁶_____ for all the cars and buses which pass through.
Yours faithfully,
Sue Davies

3 GRAMMAR PRODUCTION (5 marks)

Read the following conversation. Complete the second sentence in each pair so that it means the same as the first sentence.

1 A The road is so narrow that cars cannot park here.

   The road is too narrow ___*for cars to park here.*___

2 B They ought to make it wider at this point

   It is _____

3 A There is too little space here to make the road wider.

   There isn't _____

4 B It is possible to cut down a lot of the trees on both sides.

   A lot of _____

5 A But there aren't enough trees here in any case.

   But there are too _____

6 B Even a few trees can make it too dark for drivers to see clearly.

   Even a few trees can make it so dark _____

4 VOCABULARY (10 marks)

Read the following paragraph carefully.

The world's oceans are so vast that they can cope with the present levels of **pollution**. However, little is known about the long-term **effects** of such slow poisoning. The most serious **problem** of modern times is that man is destroying the earth's natural **resources** and **transforming** huge areas into **wasteland**. As a result, it is becoming extremely difficult to grow enough to feed the world's rapidly increasing **population**. A way of **protecting** all the **wildlife** on the earth must also be found as many species are in danger of disappearing completely from the face of the earth. The dangers, however, are not confined solely to the land and the sea. The smoke in the **atmosphere**, for example, is increasing so much that the amount of sunlight has been reduced in many cities. Man's whole **environment** is being changed in a serious way.

For each of the following dictionary definitions, write down the correct word (printed in **bold** type) in the passage.

1 birds, animals, fish which are not tame   ___*wildlife*___

2 keeping something safe from harm   _____

3 the process of making something dirty
   or impure   _____

4   barren area, desert   _____

5   the air, water and land in which we live   _____

6   completely changing in form or nature   _____

7   wealth, goods or products people can use   _____

8   the air surrounding the earth   _____

9   the number of people living in a place   _____

10   difficulty which needs attention and
thought   _____

11   results, consequences   _____

5 READING (10 marks)

Read the following passage. Write true (T) or false (F) for each of the sentences below, according to the information given. If the information is not given, put a question mark (?).

A combination of sewage, salt, air pollution, sun, sand and wind may destroy the huge statue on the outskirts of Cairo. This statue of the sun god has the body of a lion and the face of a human being. It is five thousand years old, but it is too badly damaged to be completely saved.

The statue has already been dug out of the sand three times. However, the latest problems are much more serious. First, there are no proper drains and water pipes in the neighbourhood and the underground passages round the statue have become blocked. Too much water has been running into the stone statue for several years. As a result, tiny pieces of salt have been left on the stone and have damaged it.

Secondly, air pollution from the increasing amount of traffic in Cairo is also destroying the ancient statue. The air is so full of poisonous gases that it is making the stone crumble and decay even faster.

Thirdly, the statue is being damaged by extremes of temperature. For example, although the air is very cold at night, during the day the stone of the statue becomes very hot under the strong sun. Other natural forces such as severe sandstorms also attack the statue.

Finally, the tourists who visit the statue every day also cause a lot of damage.

1 ⟦?⟧ The statue of the sun god was built for religious reasons.

2 ☐ The statue is in the centre of Cairo.

3 ☐ Part of the statue looks like a lion and part like a person.

4 ☐ The statue was built 5,000 years ago.

5 ☐ People have covered the statue with sand on three occasions in the past in order to save it.

6 ☐ The underground passages round the statue are full of waste and water.

7 ☐ Small pieces of salt have been put on the stone of the statue to prevent further damage.

8 ☐ Cars, buses and lorries have polluted the air near the statue.

9 ☐ High temperatures damage stone far more than low temperatures.

10 ☐ People have used the statue to hide from their attackers in the past.

11 ☐ Fortunately, little damage is caused by visitors to the statue.

6 READING (10 marks)

**Read the paragraphs below and the summary which follows. Complete the summary
by writing the correct word in each blank. (Write one word only.)**

Air pollution is a cause of ill-health in human beings. In a lot of countries there are laws limiting the
amount of smoke which factories can produce. Although there isn't enough information on the effects
of smoke in the atmosphere, doctors have proved that air pollution causes lung diseases.

The gases from the exhausts of cars have also increased air pollution in most cities. The lead in petrol
produces a poisonous gas which often collects in busy streets surrounded by high buildings. Children
who live in areas where there is a lot of lead in the atmosphere cannot think as quickly as other
children and are clumsy when they use their hands.

There are other long-term effects of pollution. If the gases in the atmosphere continue to increase, the
earth's climate may become warmer. A lot of the ice near the Poles may melt and may cause serious
floods.

Air ¹___*pollution*___ can make people ²_____ . Consequently, some countries

pass ³_____ to control the quantity of ⁴_____ in the air.

⁵_____ causes particular damage to the body by harming the

⁶_____ . ⁷_____ should not be used in petrol because it is bad for

children's ⁸_____ and makes them clumsy in using their hands. Poisonous gas from

⁹_____ collects in those parts of cities where there are tall buildings. Pollution can

also have an influence on the earth's ¹⁰_____ . The ice may melt near the North and

South Poles, resulting in very bad ¹¹_____ .

HUMOUR

1 GRAMMAR RECOGNITION (10 marks)

Read the following story. Put a circle round the letter of the correct word to use in each blank.

One evening Dr Peterson was at a party. A woman came up to him and began to talk about her back.

'It's very painful ¹____ I've worked for a long time in my garden,' the woman said.

   'You've hurt it ²____ for too long,' Dr Peterson replied.

He then showed her ³____ to do some exercises.

However, ⁴____ the woman left he felt very angry. He went up to a friend of his who was a lawyer.

He told him all about ⁵____ the woman and asked him for his advice.

   'Do you think I ⁶____ to send her a bill?' he asked.

The lawyer thought for a moment and nodded.

   'How much should I charge ⁷____ giving her all that advice?' Dr Peterson asked.

   'Charge her your usual fee,' the lawyer said.

The next day Dr Peterson sent the woman a bill. ⁸____, a few days later he was surprised ⁹____ a

letter from the lawyer. ¹⁰____ he opened the letter, he saw the following brief note:

   'Please find a bill for £50 for the advice ¹¹____.'

1 (A) because   B for   C by   D as soon as
2 A to bend   B by bending   C for bending   D owing to you bend
3 A what   B why   C what   D how
4 A when   B because   C if   D for
5 A meet   B meeting   C to meet   D he met
6 A should   B had better   C ought   D must
7 A by   B because of   C owing to   D for
8 A However   B In addition   C Therefore   D Alternatively
9 A by receiving   B to receive   C for receiving   D receive
10 A Because   B when   C Until   D For
11 A gave you   B what I gave you   C which gave you   D I gave you

2 GRAMMAR PRODUCTION (5 marks)

Read the following jokes and write one word or more in each blank.

1 ' _Why_ don't you take a bus home?'
'No, thanks. My mother would make me bring it back.'

2 '_____ did you get that black eye?'
'By asking too many questions.'

3 '_____ is the quickest way to the hospital.'
'Close your eyes and cross this busy street. You'll be at the hospital in ten minutes.'

4 '_____ a marvellous painting! What is it?'
'It's the place where I clean my brushes.'

5 'Waiter! _____ this a fly in my soup?'
'Don't worry, sir. There's no extra charge.'

6 'Excuse me, sir. Can you tell me _____ you've written on my composition?'
'Certainly. I told you to write more clearly.'

3 GRAMMAR PRODUCTION (5 marks)

Read the following letters and write one word or more in each blank.

Dear Mum,
    I'm writing this short letter ¹ _to_ tell you that I have arrived safely. Please write and ask for my address ² _____ you don't know it. I promise to send it straight to you as ³ _____ as I hear from you.
                    Love,
                        Ken

Dear Ken,
    I'm sending this letter to the new address ⁴ _____ you haven't given me yet. I am writing very slowly ⁵ _____ I know you are a slow reader. I hope you are still well. I'm also sending you an extra sock ⁶ _____ your father says you've grown another foot in the past few months.
                    Love, Mum

4 VOCABULARY (10 marks)

Write the correct word in each blank. A dash (—) is shown for each missing letter and some letters are given in each word.

1 'I can't stop laughing. There are some excellent j _o_ _k_ _e_ s in this magazine.'

2 'Yes, I also like the c__rt_____s by Gibbs. He's very funny and he's an excellent artist, too.'

3 'I like his sense of h__m_____. He's never unkind.'

4 'Yes, I b_____t out laughing when I saw his book.'

5 'It's very f_____y. I couldn't stop laughing, either.'

6 'Have you heard Gibbs speak? He's very w____ty.'

7 'Yes, he is. He sometimes gives lectures. I must say all his lectures are very a_____ing.'

8 'In his last lecture he talked about a pr____t__c____ joke he played when he was a student. He pretended to be a general with a wooden leg.'

9 'He's made a couple of films; both are c__m__d____s.'

10 'Yes, I enjoyed them a lot. I envy him. I wish I could make people l_____h.'

11 'Do you know any good r__d_____s?'
'Yes, what's black and white and red (read) all over?'
'A newspaper.'

5 READING (5 marks)

Each of the following newspaper extracts contains one misprint. Choose the word containing the misprint and write out the correct word in the blank on the right.

1 The man said that the (wife) he had bought was bad.   _____wine_____

2 The glass in the City Park is now very yellow because of the dry weather.   _____

3 Bramhope Wanderers hope that their best player, Sam Long, is now fat enough to play in the team.   _____

4 Several people in the Garden Restaurant were ill after eating vegetable soap.   _____

5 The burglar broke the window and climbed into the house. Suddenly he saw a polite dog in front of him.   _____

6 'Go on! Shoot!' the crowd shouted, as Lee paused with his foot on the ball. He did, and it produced a goat.   _____

6 READING (10 marks)

Read the passage below. Write the correct word in each blank.

British humour is often difficult to ¹ **understand**. A lot of ²_____ depends on the use of

³_____ which sound the ⁴_____ but have different meanings. For example, when

someone said he was on a seafood diet, everyone thought that the person ⁵_____ fish.

When he was asked what ⁶_____ of seafood he ate, however, the ⁷_____ replied,

'It's very simple indeed. When I ⁸_____ food, I eat it. That's a see-food ⁹_____ .'

   People often begin to ¹⁰_____ jokes by saying. 'Have you ¹¹_____ the one

about . . .?'

7 READING (5 marks)

Read the following extracts from newspapers. Something is wrong with six of them. Put a
cross (X) by the six odd extracts in the boxes provided.

1 ☐ Plans are being made to build a new bridge over the River Thames about ten miles south
of Abingdon.

2 ☒ Over the last three miles the two athletes ran shoulder to shoulder, with Haddon always a
yard in front of Peres.

3 ☐ A man is now recovering after the fatal crash in Bilton Road.

4 ☐ Sixteen prisoners were injured when they attempted to escape over the wall of Purley
prison yesterday.

5 ☐ Civil servants plan to go on strike in June.

6 ☐ Wanted: man to wash dishes and two waitresses.

7 ☐ A new scheme may reduce pollution from power stations if the present tests are successful,
the government announced today.

8 ☐ Do not give the baby a dirty feeding-bottle. When the baby has finished its bottle, put it in
a saucepan of water and boil it.

9 ☐ Ken Hickson scored the winning goal for Everton in their match against Arsenal in the
semi-finals last night.

10 ☐ The other driver said that Mr Petra smelled of wine. So did a policeman.

11 ☐ Alan Fletcher was elected chairman. Members of the club said they could not find a
better man.

TEST 5

ASTROLOGY

1 GRAMMAR RECOGNITION (10 marks)

Read the following predictions for people who are born between January 21st and February 18th (under the sign of Aquarius). Put a circle round the letter of the correct word or words to use in each blank.

AQUARIUS (Jan 21 – Feb 18)

People ^{1}___ those who ^{2}___ under the sign of Aquarius. No one is more generous than you are. However, your friends ^{3}___ this, and someone you like a lot may want ^{4}___ money from you. Be very careful! Soon there ^{5}___ changes at work; you may be offered a better job. ^{6}___ success go to your head! There may be health problems later in the year, and so you ^{7}___ too hard. Until May, you ^{8}___ too busy with work ^{9}___ much attention to your family. In June, however, the New Moon will signal an improvement in your family life and better relationships with those you ^{10}___.

In July a friend you haven't seen for along time will visit you. You ^{11}___ abroad on business or for a holiday towards the end of the year.

1 A do not always understand   B would not always understand
   C are not always understanding   D not always understand
2 A born   B be born   C are born   D did born
3 A know   B do know   C are knowing   D would know
4 A borrow   B borrowing   C to borrow   D for borrowing
5 A would be   B are being   C have been   D will be
6 A You not let   B Not let   C Don't let   D Never be letting
7 A don't work   B aren't working   C haven't worked   D shouldn't work
8 A will be   B are being   C are   D can be
9 A pay   B to pay   C paying   D for paying
10 A are loving   B love   C will love   D loved
11 A are travelling   B travelled   C would travel   D will travel

2 GRAMMAR PRODUCTION (10 marks)

Read the following horoscope and use a suitable form of each verb in bold type. Write your answers in the blanks.

There (¹**be**) _____ *are* _____ twelve animal signs in Chinese astrology. Each year (²**rule**) _____ by one of twelve animals: the rat, the ox, the tiger, the rabbit, etc. For example, 1987 (³**be**) _____ the year of the rabbit, and the next year of the rabbit (⁴**be**) _____ 1999. Each animal (⁵**have**) _____ certain characteristics – for example, the tiger (⁶**appear**) _____ very restless and brave; you can never tell what he or she (⁷**do**) _____ . A baby who is born in the year of the rabbit (⁸**grow up**) _____ to lead a calm and peaceful life. As a monkey (⁹**learn**) _____ things quickly, a person born in the year of the monkey (¹⁰**succeed**) _____ in whatever he or she (¹¹**do**) _____ .

3 VOCABULARY (10 marks)

Read the following sentences and write the correct word in each blank. Choose the words from the list below.

> predictions   travel   career   horoscope   opportunities
> astrology   romance   influence   changes   sign   birthday

A   Have you seen your ¹ *horoscope* in today's paper?

B   No, I haven't. I'm not interested in ²_____ .

A   What's your birth ³_____ ?

B   It's Aries. My ⁴_____ is on April 4th.

A   It says here Venus will be under the ⁵_____ of Saturn. There'll be plenty of

   ⁶_____ to see different places as it's a good time for ⁷_____ . Oh

   dear. It says there'll be ⁸_____ at work that may affect your ⁹_____ .

   Don't worry. You'll meet a dark stranger and find ¹⁰_____ .

B   I don't believe anyone can make such ¹¹_____ !

4 READING (10 marks)

Read the following predictions. Write true (T) or false (F) for each of the sentences below, according to the information given. If the information is not given, put a question mark (?).

Capricorn (Dec 22 – Jan 20) Friends will make you angry this week. Try to understand the reason for their behaviour and be patient. You will get something which you have long wanted.

Aquarius (Jan 21 – Feb 19) Uranus crosses the path of Mars. It means you will have to work harder if you want to succeed in your work. Wait for a few weeks before you start anything new.

Pisces (Feb 20 – Mar 20) This is a good time for romance. A stranger will walk into your life. But don't forget old friends. A lot will depend on how you treat the people who love you.

Aries (Mar 21 – Apr 20) Stay in bed this week! You will quarrel with your friends and you will feel sad and depressed. A mistake may cost you a lot of money.

Taurus (Apr 21 – May 21) The morning star shines with a special light now. It is the time to do new things. If you want to move house or change your job, start making plans now.

Gemini (May 22 – Jun 21) You will have too much to do both at work and at home this week. Don't be in a hurry. Friends will help you if you are not too proud to accept their help.

Cancer (Jun 22 – Jul 23) The force of Mars entering your star sign will give you a lot of energy. Be determined to finish whatever you start to do this week.

Leo (Jul 24 – Aug 23) There may be one or two small quarrels at home but they will not be important. Listen to your family's advice. Good news later will make you happy.

Virgo (Aug 24 – Sep 23) This is a good week to make travel plans, especially if you are going abroad. Someone near you will want to travel with you and will be able to help you.

Libra (Sep 24 – Oct 23) You will receive some money, but be very careful. Don't lend it to anyone. Something may happen that will waste your time.

Scorpio (Oct 24 – Nov 22) The full moon will affect your life this week. You could be promoted in your job or win a competition. The week will be full of excitement.

Sagittarius (Nov 23 – Dec 21) This week may be fairly busy at work but your home life will be full of peace and happiness. Don't refuse any help which anyone offers you.

1 [T] This week friends will offer to help people born under the star sign of Gemini.

2 ☐ Someone whose birthday is on August 14th was born under the star sign Leo.

3 ☐ The week for people born at the end of October will be dull.

4 ☐ Mars will help to give Cancerians a lot of energy this week.

5 ☐ Pisces people will meet someone they don't know this week.

6 ☐ People with the star sign Gemini are usually very proud.

7 ☐ If you are a Leo, you should listen to suggestions from your family this week.

8 ☐ People born under Taurus shouldn't make plans to do anything new.

9 ☐ Sagittarians will have a lot of quarrels at home.

10 ☐ If you were born at the end of March, you must be careful or you may lose both friends and money.

11 ☐ People born at the beginning of January are advised to be patient with their friends.

5 READING (10 marks)

Read the following letters written to and from an astrologer. Every twelfth word is missing. Read *both* letters and then write the correct word in each blank.

Dear Professor Zodiac,

    I was born on October 5th, 1973 at 8.27 pm in Kuwait. I should be very grateful if you could answer the following ¹ *questions* :

1. Will I change my job ?
2. When will I get ² _____ ?
3. Will I travel abroad in the near future ?
4. Will I become ³ _____ later in my life ?

                    Anna Wright

Dear Anna,

    According to your ⁴ _____ signs, you must be patient and not rush into changing your ⁵ _____ yet. However, Uranus, the planet of freedom, will have a great ⁶ _____ on your life next year and your application for a new ⁷ _____ will succeed.

    In May this year a stranger will enter your ⁸ _____ . You will soon fall deeply in love and be very happy, ⁹ _____ be careful and don't rush into marriage.

    When you reach the ¹⁰ _____ of thirty, you will travel abroad frequently on business. Yes, your ¹¹ _____ show that you will earn a lot of money and become very rich when you are middle-aged.

                Professor Zodiac

AIR TRAVEL

1 GRAMMAR RECOGNITION (10 marks)

Read the following paragraphs taken from an airline ticket. Put a circle round the letter of the correct word or words to use in each blank.

Baggage

First Class or Business Class passengers will be allowed up to thirty kilogrammes of baggage. ¹____ other passengers will be allowed up to twenty kilogrammes.

   In addition, ²____ passenger will be allowed to carry ³____ piece of hand baggage which is not more than 115 cms in total dimension. ⁴____ articles which will be carried free of charge are: a lady's handbag, a blanket, books for reading during the flight, baby food, a baby's carrying basket, an umbrella, and a camera. Passengers who travel First Class will also be allowed to take with them ⁵____ bag for clothes.

   ⁶____ hand baggage must be placed under the seat or in the overhead locker.

   Name labels should be put on every ⁷____, and all ⁸____ labels should be removed. Bags should be locked, and ⁹____ important papers, medicines, cash and jewellery should be taken in hand baggage.

   Every ¹⁰____ must go through a security check before boarding the plane and ¹¹____ knives and weapons (whether real or toys) will be removed.

1 A Each   B Every   Ⓒ All   D One
2 A Single   B All   C Other   D Each
3 A one   B every   C each   D other
4 A Other   B All   C Another   D Few
5 A other   B each other   C another   D the other
6 A Some   B A   C One   D All
7 A baggage   B piece of baggage   C baggages   D pieces of baggage
8 A the   B other   C of the   D every other
9 A all   B each of   C all of   · D other of
10 A of the passenger   B passenger   C passengers   D of the passengers
11 A every   B all of   C all   D every of

2 GRAMMAR PRODUCTION (10 marks)

Read the following timetable and then write one word in each blank in the passage below.

London to	Mon	Tue	Wed	Thu	Fri	Sat	Sun	Depart	Flight	Cost
Abu Dhabi			✓					15 30	BA 011	£896
				✓			✓	13 00	BA 033	..
	✓							16 35	BA 033	..
			✓		✓			21 45	BA 011	..
Amman		✓	✓	✓	✓	✓	✓	15 30	BA 157	£629
Cairo	✓	✓	✓	✓	✓	✓	✓	15 40	BA 155	£627
Dubai	✓	✓	✓	✓	✓	✓	✓	10 15	BA 147	£896
Khartoum		✓			✓			09 30	BA 153	£797

There is a flight [1] _**every**_ day from London to Abu Dhabi except on Saturday. Four of [2] _____

flights leave London in the afternoon but the [3] _____ flights leave in the evening. There are

flights to Amman on [4] _____ days and [5] _____ of them leave London at 15 30. There are

flights [6] _____ day of the week to Cairo and Dubai. The flights [7] _____ Dubai leave

in [8] _____ middle of the morning. On two mornings [9] _____ week there are flights to

Khartoum.

[10] _____ of the fares to the Middle East costs more than £1,000, and the ordinary return fare

to Dubai is [11] _____ same as that to Abu Dhabi.

3 VOCABULARY (10 marks)

Write the correct word in each blank. A dash (—) is shown for each missing letter and some
letters are given in each word.

Don't leave your seat until the [1]a _**i r**_ cr _**a f t**_ has taxied to a halt. Then pick up any hand

[2]b __ gg __ g __ which you have and leave the plane. Once in the [3]t __ rm __ n __ l building, follow the

sign [4]'A __ __ __ v __ ls' and go straight to the [5]i __ __ __ gr __ t __ __ n area.

After your [6]p __ __ __ p __ __ t and visa have been checked, go to the baggage collection area to

[7]cl __ __ __ your bags and cases. If you have a lot of cases, find a [8]tr __ ll __ __ to put them on. Next

take them through the [9]C __ st __ __ __ . If you have wine or jewellery, you must [10]d __ cl __ __ __

them and pay [11]d __ t __ on them.

4 READING (6 marks)
Read the paragraph. Every seventh word is missing. Write the correct word in each blank.

There are now very few plane crashes. Driving a car is far more ¹ *dangerous* than flying in

a modern passenger ²_____ . However, if an aircraft does actually ³_____ , most

people on board will probably ⁴_____ killed. Many accidents are caused by ⁵_____

and not aircraft faults. The most ⁶_____ form of pilot error is ⁷_____ too soon before

the plane reaches the airport runway. Moreover, certain airports are much more dangerous than others.

5 READING (8 marks)
Read the following paragraphs about booking a flight.

When you want to book a flight to a certain place, visit your nearest travel agent. Tell the travel agent the date when you want to travel and the destination to which you want to go. The travel agent will then type this information into a small computer. After checking everything on the computer screen, he/she will send this information to a central computer. This central computer contains all information about bookings and destinations, and sends a reply, showing which are the most suitable flights. It also shows whether the flights are fully booked or not. The information which is now shown on the small computer screen is continually changing as other bookings are made in other parts of the world.

   The travel agent now types in your booking. Then the computer will ask for your name and address as well as for certain other information. It will also ask how you will pay for your ticket (by cheque or by credit card). Next, the computer confirms the booking and makes a request for payment. When you have paid for your ticket, the travel agent types this information into the computer as well. Finally, some computers print out a ticket before you leave the travel agent's.

Now put the following sentences in their correct order. Write the appropriate number for each sentence in the box provided.

A [5] Details about the flights and seats available are sent back.

B [ ] The computer then wants information about the method of payment.

C [ ] The tickets are issued either at that time or later.

D [ ] The computer asks for personal details.

E [ ] Make your request to the travel agent and give him/her all the details.

F [4] Your request is then checked and sent to the main computer.

G [ ] Go to a travel agent.

H [ ] The computer asks for payment.

I [ ] The travel agent feeds your initial request into a small computer.

J [6] The booking is typed into the small computer.

K [ ] The booking is confirmed.

6 READING (6 marks)

Read the following notes about three modern aircraft and then complete the sentences which follow. Write one word or more in each blank.

FOKKER 50
Wing span: 29 m
Length: 25.19 m
Cruising speed 515 km/h
Passengers: 46 – 60

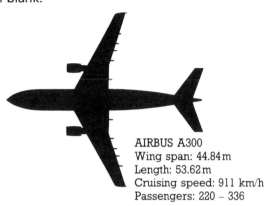

AIRBUS A300
Wing span: 44.84 m
Length: 53.62 m
Cruising speed: 911 km/h
Passengers: 220 – 336

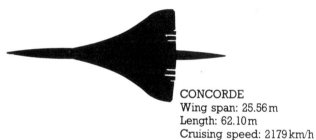

CONCORDE
Wing span: 25.56 m
Length: 62.10 m
Cruising speed: 2179 km/h
Passengers: 100

BOEING 737
Wing span: 28.90 m
Length: 33.40 m
Cruising speed: 889 km/h
Passengers: Up to 149

1 The ___Airbus___ is the largest plane.

2 The _____ can carry more passengers than the Boeing 737.

3 The _____ can fly more than twice as fast as the Airbus.

4 _____ of the planes are more than fifty metres long.

5 The plane which carries the _____ number of passengers is the Fokker 50.

6 The _____ and the _____ have almost the same cruising speeds.

7 The plane with the _____ wing span flies the fastest.

SURVEYS

1 GRAMMAR RECOGNITION (10 marks)

Put a circle round the letter of the correct word or words to use in each blank.

According to a recent survey, most Chinese in Hong Kong preferred to work for Americans. They said that during the past ten years or so American businesses ¹___ well and were very friendly. Almost all of them who had worked for Americans said they ²___ happy in their work.

They were then asked ³___ they liked working for American bosses. Most replied ⁴___ they were usually fair, kind, friendly and generous.

When asked whether ⁵___ working for British bosses, however, the Chinese ⁶___ that the British bosses were too strict and proud.

The survey ⁷___ among 200 Chinese managers and advanced business students in Hong Kong. Most of the people ⁸___ said that the working conditions were also much better in American companies.

When managers were asked ⁹___ they often conducted business, they replied that they ¹⁰___ to tea houses. A few people said that ¹¹___ business with Americans over lunch at expensive hotel restaurants.

```
 1  A  pay      B  will pay     C  are paying    (D) paid
 2  A  are      B  will be      C  have been     D  were
 3  A  that     B  if    C  about     D  why
 4  A  to       B  that     C  if     D  about
 5  A  did they like     B  they liked     C  they did like     D  liked they
 6  A  answer      B  will answer     C  answered     D  have answered
 7  A  conducted      B  was conducted     C  has conducted     D  was conducting
 8  A  interview      B  to interview     C  interviewed     D  interviewing
 9  A  where     B  when     C  how     D  if
10  A  are going      B  have gone     C  went     D  will go
11  A  they had often done      C  had they often done
    B  they often had done      D  often had they done
```

2 GRAMMAR PRODUCTION (10 marks)

Read the following survey of road accidents. Complete the report of the survey by writing in each blank the correct pronoun, e.g. (*he, they, we*), and the appropriate verb in the correct tense.

'We have examined over 1,200 accidents while conducting our survey. 87% of all these accidents are caused by drivers' carelessness. Only 9% of the accidents examined by us result from mechanical faults in vehicles. Our survey clearly shows that a large number of accidents can be prevented. Moreover, many of the drivers questioned have given very foolish reasons for the cause of the accidents. "The pedestrian had no idea where to go, and so I ran over him," one driver said.'

The people who conducted the survey said that they ¹ *had examined* over 1,200

accidents and that 87% of all those accidents ²_____ by drivers' carelessness. They

added that only 9% of the accidents examined by ³_____ ⁴_____

from mechanical faults in vehicles. ⁵_____ survey clearly ⁶_____ that

a large number of accidents ⁷_____ . Moreover, many of the drivers

questioned ⁸_____ very foolish reasons for the cause of the accidents.

One driver had said that a pedestrian ⁹_____ no idea where to go and so

¹⁰_____ ¹¹_____ over him.

3 VOCABULARY (10 marks)

Read the following paragraph about opinion polls.

People often laugh at opinion polls and remember times when they were slightly incorrect. However, they often forget all the times when they were accurate. A poll should be conducted very carefully and should sample a cross-section of the population. The cross-section should be selected very carefully so that the right balance of ages, sexes and social classes can be achieved. At first it was very difficult for many people to accept that a sample of one or two thousand could reflect accurately the views of millions, but polls have now proved themselves. However, polls should not claim to do what they are not intended to do. The findings should always be examined very carefully before predictions are made with any degree of certainty.

Which words in the paragraph can be replaced by the words below? Write the correct word from the paragraph in each blank.

1	mixture	*cross-section*	7	carried out	_____
2	chosen	_____	8	results	_____
3	meant	_____	9	opinions	_____
4	a little	_____	10	wrong	_____
5	forecasts	_____	11	studied	_____
6	represent	_____			

4 READING (8 marks)

Read the following results of a survey of factors which sixty people think are important in choosing a job. The numbers in the table are the numbers of people giving the factor a particular place or grade from 1st to 10th.

	Most important ⟶ Least important									
	1st	2nd	3rd	4th	5th	6th	7th	8th	9th	10th
1 Pleasant surroundings	2	4	12	10	9	8	2	6	7	–
2 Challenging and interesting work	34	11	1	4	5	2	2	–	–	1
3 Wages	11	16	7	11	4	2	1	3	4	1
4 Ease of job (not tiring)	3	2	2	2	–	10	17	10	8	6
5 Opportunities for travel	8	8	8	10	7	6	3	6	4	–
6 Job security	–	1	1	3	2	5	2	8	9	29
7 Job prestige	1	3	10	8	6	5	7	7	9	4
8 Benefit to community	6	5	8	6	11	7	7	4	1	5
9 Opportunities to meet people	2	6	2	2	9	9	10	11	4	5
10 Parent's wishes	1	4	3	4	3	6	9	5	14	11

Write true (T) or false (F) for each of the sentences below, according to the information in the table. If the information is not in the table, put a question mark (?).

1 ☑ T Opportunities for travel were given as the most important reason in choosing a job for eight people out of the sixty.

2 ☐ Most of the people interviewed in the survey said that challenging and interesting work was their first reason in choosing a particular job.

3 ☐ Most people thought that the chance to travel was the least important reason for choosing a job.

4 ☐ Eleven people thought that wages were the second most important reason in choosing a job.

5 ☐ Pleasant surroundings were not such an important factor in choosing a job as most offices were quite comfortable.

6 ☐ A lot of people thought it was most important to see how easy or difficult a job was before choosing it.

7 ☐ On the whole parents' wishes were not an important factor in determining the choice of a job.

8 ☐ Those people who chose a job because of the wages did not think that benefit to the community was important.

9 ☐ Job security appeared to be the least important factor in choosing a job.

5 READING (12 marks)

The table below gives the results of a survey about the kind of society people say we are living in. For example, 86% of the people interviewed think we are becoming more aggressive while only 4% think we are becoming less aggressive. (The other 10% think we are neither more nor less aggressive than in the past.)

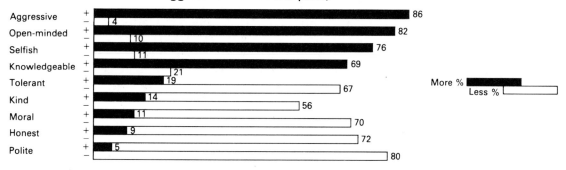

Write one or two words or a figure in each blank for numbers 1 to 10.

A surprising 86% of all the people interviewed believe we are more ¹ *aggressive* now than ten years ago. 82% think that we are becoming more ² _____ , although ³ _____ think the reverse. Over three-quarters of the people interviewed feel that other people are becoming increasingly ⁴ _____ . ⁵ _____ also think we are becoming harder and less generous to others while 14% disagreed. 70% think that ⁶ _____ are less strict now and look back with envy on the past. Only 11% disagreed with them. 72% think that people are now ⁷ _____ honest while even more think that courtesy is quickly disappearing. Only ⁸ _____ thought that people were actually more polite than ten years ago. However, there is one fact which is difficult to understand. Why do 69% believe we are more ⁹ _____ if almost as many believe we are less ¹⁰ _____ ? To understand all is to forgive all, said one philosopher.

Circle the letter of the correct answer.

11 Many think that people's behaviour and values are _____ .
    A improving   B the same as before   Ⓒ getting worse   D old-fashioned

12 Knowledge usually encourages _____ .
    A honesty   B tolerance   C selfishness   D morals

13 The findings of the survey show a great deal of _____ .
    A hope   B friendliness   C pride   D pessimism

14 The survey tells us what sort of people we _____ .
    A shouldn't be   B think we are   C want to be   D hope to be

REVISION TEST

1 GRAMMAR RECOGNITION (10 marks)

Read the following paragraphs about a survey. Put a circle round the letter of the correct word or words to use in each blank.

In a recent survey ¹____ by Leisurama, 150 travel agents ²____ to solve certain holiday problems. As a result, it ³____ that most travel agents frequently give inaccurate information and unsound advice. They simply did not know ⁴____ about the places that they recommended.

When a tourist asked a travel agent ⁵____ a hotel on the Greek island of Corfu, the travel agent booked a hotel on the island of Kos, 500 miles away. When they ⁶____ for advice about crossing the Adriatic Sea from Italy to Corfu, several travel agents said it ⁷____ impossible to go by sea. Two others suggested ⁸____ all the way round to the Greek mainland.

Many agents didn't know whether visas ⁹____ for certain countries and some didn't even know ¹⁰____ the local money was called.

Leisurama said that they often received better advice from students who were able to use ¹¹____ the reference books and guides which were available.

```
 1  A conduct     B conducting   (C) conducted     D to conduct
 2  A were inviting   B invited    C inviting      D were invited
 3  A found      B was found    C finds      D was finding
 4  A enough     B too      C very      D so
 5  A recommending   B recommend    C to recommend    D recommended
 6  A were asked    B asked     C asking     D were asking
 7  A is being    B has been    C will be     D was
 8  A to drive    B drive     C for driving    D driving
 9  A requires    B are required   C were required   D required
10  A what      B how     C whether     D where
11  A all      B every     C any      D each
```

2 GRAMMAR PRODUCTION (10 marks)

Read the following paragraph about future air travel. There is one word missing from each line. Put an oblique stroke (/) where the word has been omitted and write the missing word in each blank. Write one word only.

Answer key

TEST 1

1 1 D 2 A 3 B 4 A 5 B 6 B 7 B 8 C 9 D 10 C 11 A

2 1 being 2 seeing 3 travelling 4 to get 5 to work 6 concentrating
7 to go 8 apply/should apply 9 to apply 10 to study 11 applying

3 1 A 2 A 3 C 4 A 5 B 6 C

4 1 teaches 2 lectures 3 explains 4 learns 5 shows 6 describes

5 1 teaching 2 try/practise 3 test/examination 4 class/group 5 beginners
6 practice 7 learnt/learned/studied/acquired 8 knowledge 9 level 10 speak/talk
11 lectures/talks

6 1 T 2 ? 3 T 4 T 5 ? 6 F 7 T 8 F 9 T 10 T 11 T

TEST 2

1 1 D 2 A 3 B 4 C 5 C 6 D 7 D 8 A 9 A 10 C 11 A

2 1 are collected 2 takes 3 are stamped 4 are sorted 5 being sent 6 delivers

3 1 is measured 2 is washed 3 is put/is placed 4 is covered/is mixed
5 is cooked/is heated/is boiled 6 is taken/is lifted

4 1 description 2 First 3 Afterwards 4 turn 5 eventually 6 Finally

5 1 B 2 D 3 C 4 A 5 B 6 A

6 1 E 2 C 3 F 4 B 5 D 6 A

7 1 B 2 G 3 C 4 F 5 E 6 A 7 D

8 1 cane 2 Next/Then/Afterwards 3 crystals 4 done/achieved 5 revolves/turns/spins
6 sap 7 sugar 8 transported/shipped/taken/carried 9 extracted/separated/obtained
10 make/produce/manufacture 11 Nothing/Little

TEST 3

1 1 too 2 so much 3 so/so much 4 so many 5 enough 6 too 7 enough 8 too
many 9 enough 10 too 11 too

2 1 so 2 that 3 enough 4 too 5 so 6 enough

3 1 for cars to park here 2 is too narrow at this point
3 enough space here to make the road wider 4 the trees can be cut down on both sides *or* the trees on
both sides can be cut down 5 few trees here in any case 6 that drivers can't/cannot see clearly

4 1 wildlife 2 protecting 3 pollution 4 wasteland 5 environment 6 transforming
7 resources 8 atmosphere 9 population 10 problem 11 effects

5 1 ? 2 F 3 T 4 T 5 ? 6 T 7 F 8 T 9 ? 10 ? 11 F

6 1 pollution 2 ill 3 laws 4 smoke 5 Air pollution 6 lungs 7 Lead 8 brains/health
9 lead/exhausts 10 climate 11 floods

TEST 4

1 1 A 2 B 3 D 4 A 5 B 6 C 7 D 8 A 9 B 10 B 11 D

2 1 Why 2 How 3 Which/What 4 What 5 Is 6 what

3 1 to 2 if 3 soon 4 which 5 as/since/because 6 as/since/because

4 1 jokes 2 cartoons 3 humour 4 burst 5 funny 6 witty 7 amusing 8 practical
9 comedies 10 laugh 11 riddles

5 1 wine 2 grass 3 fit 4 soup 5 police 6 goal

6 1 understand 2 humour/wit 3 words 4 same 5 ate 6 kind/sort/type 7 man/person
8 see 9 diet 10 tell/crack 11 heard

7 2, 3, 6, 8, 10 and 11 are wrong

TEST 5

1 1 A 2 C 3 A 4 C 5 D 6 C 7 D 8 A 9 B 10 B 11 D

2 1 are 2 is ruled 3 was 4 will be 5 has 6 appears 7 will do 8 will grow up
9 learns 10 will succeed 11 does

3 1 horoscope 2 astrology 3 sign 4 birthday 5 influence 6 opportunities 7 travel
8 changes 9 career 10 romance 11 predictions

4 1 T 2 T 3 F 4 T 5 T 6 ? 7 T 8 F 9 F 10 T 11 T

5 1 questions 2 married 3 rich 4 star/birth/zodiac 5 life/job 6 influence 7 job
8 life 9 but 10 age 11 stars

TEST 6

1 1 C 2 D 3 A 4 A 5 C 6 D 7 B 8 B 9 A 10 B 11 C

2 1 every 2 the 3 other 4 six/most 5 all 6 every 7 to/for 8 the 9 a
10 None 11 the

3 1 aircraft 2 baggage 3 terminal 4 arrivals 5 immigration 6 passport 7 claim
8 trolley 9 Customs 10 declare 11 duty

4 i dangerous 2 plane 3 crash 4 be 5 mistakes/errors/pilots/people 6 common
7 landing

5 1 G 2 E 3 I 4 F 5 A 6 J 7 D 8 B 9 K 10 H 11 C

6 1 Airbus 2 Airbus 3 Concorde 4 Two 5 smallest/least/lowest 6 Airbus, Boeing
7 smallest/shortest

TEST 7

1 1 D 2 D 3 D 4 B 5 B 6 C 7 B 8 C 9 A 10 C 11 A

2 1 had examined 2 were caused 3 them 4 resulted 5 Their 6 showed 7 could be
prevented 8 had given 9 had/had had 10 he 11 ran/had run

3 1 cross-section 2 selected 3 intended 4 slightly 5 predictions 6 reflect 7 conducted
8 findings 9 views 10 incorrect 11 examined

4 1 T 2 T 3 F 4 F 5 ? 6 F 7 T 8 ? 9 T

5 1 aggressive 2 open-minded 3 10% 4 selfish 5 56% 6 morals 7 less 8 5%
9 knowledgeable 10 tolerant 11 C 12 B 13 D 14 B

TEST 8

1 1 C 2 D 3 B 4 A 5 C 6 A 7 D 8 D 9 C 10 A 11 A

2 1 there will be 2 which are called 3 consist of two 4 It will not 5 except for repairs
6 over another continent 7 will be used 8 to and/or from 9 will be fuelled 10 be too large
11 spend all of

3 1 humour 2 survey 3 interviewed/approached/seen 4 funny 5 laugh 6 practical

4 curriculum 5 career 2 influence 4 horoscope 1 travel 6 lecture 3

5 1 C 2 F 3 D 4 A 5 E 6 B

6 1 F 2 F 3 ? 4 F 5 T 6 T

7 1 cleaning 2 building 3 fields/wells 4 developed/grown/started/begun 5 Mediterranean
6 all 7 flow/run/drain 8 replaced/replenished 9 rivers 10 flow/run/drain
11 rubbish/pollutants

TEST 9

1 1 A 2 D 3 A 4 B 5 B 6 A 7 D 8 C 9 B 10 B 11 D

2 1 years ago the 2 However, when it 3 it was/became necessary 4 tried to do

5 this by typing   6 incorrect because there   7 comma instead of   8 sent the spacecraft
9 Venus, but the   10 dollars were wasted   11 such a mistake

3   1 computer   2 keyboard   3 function   4 socket   5 monitor   6 screen   7 programme
8 disc/disk   9 mouse   10 printer   11 joystick

4   1 afford   2 time   3 difficult   4 books   5 few   6 write   7 not/never   8 years
9 them   10 situation/position   11 know

5   1 √√   2 x   3 √   4 √   5 √√   6 x   7 x   8 √√   9 √   10 √√
11 £340

TEST 10

1   1 C   2 D   3 D   4 C   5 A   6 A   7 B   8 D   9 B   10 B   11 A
2   1 were doing   2 do not remember   3 was watching   4 was doing   5 went out   6 was
frightened   7 remember   8 calling out   9 were talking   10 heard   11 began
3   A 9   B 3   C 5   D 11   E 10   F 7   G 6   H 8   I 1   J 4   K 2
4   1 life   2 ruined/destroyed/devastated   3 death   4 mine/mines   5 earthquake/disaster
6 survived/lived   7 factories/offices   8 killed/crushed/injured/trapped   9 collapsed/fell
10 number   11 building/house
5   1 T   2 T   3 ?   4 F   5 T   6 T   7 F   8 F   9 ?   10 T   11 T

TEST 11

1   1 B   2 D   3 B   4 C   5 D   6 B   7 B   8 D   9 D   10 B   11 B
2   1 inventions are carried   2 out by scientists   3 opportunities for other   4 Britain, there is
5 programme which attempts   6 all the various   7 organising the programme   8 inventions a/per
year   9 developed by private   10 However, it is   11 it be wanted
3   1 invention   2 manufacture   3 ingenious   4 devices   5 designed   6 practical
4   1 revolutionary   2 original   3 laboratory   4 experiments   5 tests   6 patent
5   1 will   2 stores   3 a   4 is   5 where/if   6 enter/approach   7 find   8 opening/device/
'Stop-Roach'   9 tests/testing/trials/trialling   10 invention/device   11 been
6   1 cylinder   2 tinfoil   3 base   4 funnel   5 flywheel   6 handle
7   1 T   2 F   3 T   4 F   5 ?   6 T

TEST 12

1   1 B   2 B   3 A   4 B   5 D   6 A   7 B   8 C   9 A   10 D   11 B
2   1 used to be   2 called   3 used to be surrounded   4 used to grow   5 used to have   6 built
7 used to trade   8 used to lie   9 was swallowed up   10 think   11 sank   12 disappeared
3   1 customs   2 traditions   3 festivals   4 habits   5 routines   6 practice
4   1 D   2 B   3 A   4 B   5 C   6 B
5   1 a trilby   2 a fez   3 a bowler   4 a topper   5 a beret   6 a cap
     1 T   2 F   3 ?   4 F   5 F   6 T
6   1 night   2 god   3 sun   4 build/use   5 snake/serpent   6 spread/grew/developed
7 country   8 civilisation/country   9 live   10 Aztecs/people   11 Mexico/theirs

TEST 13

1   1 B   2 A   3 D   4 C   5 B   6 D   7 B   8 D   9 B   10 A   11 A
2   1 has been one   2 than had been   3 had been expected   4 sales would be   5 October to
December   6 forecast a small   7 can be attributed   8 Moreover, the sales   9 sales were of
10 products as computer   11 what had been
3   1 coordinating   2 sales   3 supply   4 finance   5 personnel   6 public relations
4   1 D   2 C   3 A   4 A   5 D   6 B

5 1 beat   2 sold/bought/purchased   3 demand/market   4 greater   5 sales   6 year
7 increase/rise   8 number   9 decreasing/declining/dropping/falling   10 rose/increased
11 jobs/posts/positions/vacancies

6

TEST 14

1 1 D   2 B   3 D   4 D   5 B   6 A   7 D   8 A   9 C   10 B   11 C
2 1 resources have taken   2 we are quickly   3 Recently a UN   4 that the world's
5 would last about   6 there would be   7 could be controlled   8 continued to grow
9 supplies   would last   10 governments must now   11 fuels that are
3 1 B   2 A   3 D   4 D   5 A   6 C   7 B   8 C   9 C   10 B   11 D
4 1 H   2 D   3 F   4 A   5 G   6 I   7 K   8 C   9 J   10 E   11 B
5 1 place/put   2 trap/use/catch/collect   3 of   4 power/heat/energy   5 than   6 built/installed/
put/placed/introduced   7 solar   8 removal/extraction/separation   9 For/With   10 not
11 methods/ways

TEST 15

1 1 D   2 D   3 A   4 D   5 C   6 B   7 A   8 A   9 D   10 D   11 C
2 1 tried/had tried   2 had called   3 would have been able   4 preventing   5 told
6 decided/had decided   7 phoning   8 had begged/begged   9 had gone off   10 would have
been   11 was hit
3 1 B   2 D   3 A   4 A   5 D   6 C   7 B   8 C   9 A   10 B   11 D
4 1 D   2 I   3 G   4 J   5 B   6 E   7 F   8 H   9 A   10 K   11 C
5 1 1983   2 cinema   3 decreased   4 traffic lights   5 offices   6 50   7 more/greater
8 accident warning signs   9 pedestrian bridge   10 1986   11 decrease

TEST 16

1 1 B   2 B   3 A   4 D   5 A   6 A   7 B   8 D   9 A   10 D   11 D
2 1 were injured   2 was carrying   3 hit   4 said   5 was travelling   6 entered   7 failed
8 to stop   9 will be held   10 were hurt   11 suffered
3 1 predicted   2 fluctuate   3 dramatic   4 demand   5 levelled   6 marked
4 1 manufactured   2 devices   3 revolution   4 programme   5 invention   6 ingenious
5 1 used   2 of   3 human   4 designs/plans/ideas   5 jobs/tasks   6 tractors   7 in   8 a
9 robots   10 like   11 design/appearance/shape/form/role
6 1 x   2 ✓   3 ✓   4 x   5 ✓   6 ✓   7 x   8 ✓   9 x   10 x   11 ✓   12 x
13 x   14 x   15 ✓   16 ✓   17 x   18 x   19 x   20 ✓   21 ✓   22 x

In the next century there/be giant 'airports' in the sky. 1 ____will____

These flying 'airports', which called spanloaders 2 _____

in America, will only consist two large wings. 3 _____

It not be necessary for these huge 'airports' to land 4 _____

on the ground except repairs. Passengers will board 5 _____

them over one continent and leave them over continent. 6 _____

Consequently, a lot of smaller planes will used to 7 _____

transfer passengers to from these flying 'airports'. 8 _____

The 'airports' will fuelled in the air and will weigh 9 _____

up to 1,500,000 kg. They will be large to land in 10 _____

ordinary airports but they will spend of the time in the sky. 11 _____

3 VOCABULARY (5 marks)

Read the following paragraph and then write the most appropriate word in each blank.

Even in the same country people differ greatly in their sense of [1] __humour__ , according to a

recent [2] _____ carried out in Britain. Over a thousand people were [3] _____ and

were told the same four jokes. While certain people found all four of the jokes very

[4] _____ , other people didn't [5] _____ at even one of the jokes. On the whole,

tricks and [6] _____ jokes were not liked by people over the age of twenty.

4 VOCABULARY (5 marks)

Read the following paragraph. The numbers stand for words which have been omitted. Write the correct number for each word in the box provided.

Aries Your [1] ____ for this week is good. You will meet someone who will help you in your future [2] ____. You will also attend an interesting [3] ____ which will have a great [4] ____ on your life. If you are still at school or college, changes in the [5] ____ will make your course more interesting. Whether you are at school or at work, there will soon be opportunities for [6] ____, so be prepared to see new places and meet new people!

[5] curriculum   ☐ travel

☐ horoscope   ☐ influence

☐ career   ☐ lecture

5 READING (5 marks)

Look at the following drawings showing the process of making papyrus, the writing material used instead of paper in the ancient world.

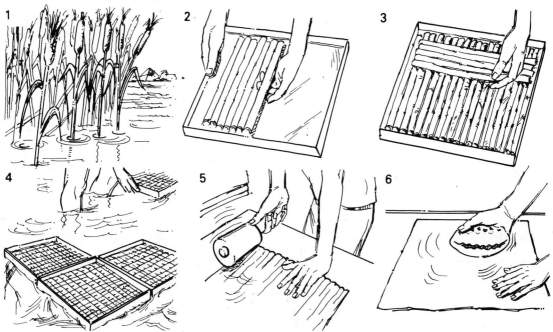

Now put the following sentences about this process in their correct order. Write the appropriate number in the box for each sentence.

A ☐ The tray which contained the reeds was then covered with water to help the reeds to stick together.

B ☐ Finally, the sheet of papyrus was polished with ivory or a smooth shell in order to remove any roughness.

C ☐ 1 Papyrus was made from the papyrus reed which grew near the Nile.

D ☐ Other strips of reed were then put across these strips.

E ☐ After the strips were stuck in this way, the sheet of papyrus was beaten with a hammer and left to dry in the sun.

F ☐ Strips of papyrus reed were laid side by side on a large tray.

6 READING (5 marks)

Read the following extract from a newspaper article. Write true (T) or false (F) for each sentence, according to the information given. If the information is not given, put a question mark (?).

Do smaller classes really help?

In an experiment in Canada, ten-year-old children were put in classes of four sizes: 16, 23, 30 and 37 children in each class. Their teachers said that the smaller classes would result in more individual attention and better marks. However, when the children were tested, those in the smaller classes didn't get higher marks than the others, except in mathematics. Moreover, pupils in the larger classes said they liked school just as much.

Perhaps the most surprising result was the difference between what teachers expected and the actual results obtained. More than 90% of the teachers expected the smaller classes to do well.

After teaching these smaller classes, over 80% of the teachers thought the pupils had done better. However, according to the researchers, nothing of the sort happened. Class size seemed to make a difference only to the teachers' own attitudes – and not to the results they obtained.

There may be three reasons for this. First, teachers may be used to teaching large classes and may not know how to get the best results from small classes. Secondly, the results of teaching pupils in small classes may take a year to show. Thirdly, even a class containing sixteen pupils is really a large class, and real improvements can only be made with classes of fewer than a dozen pupils.

1 $\boxed{F}$ The results of children in larger classes were much better than those of children in smaller classes.

2 $\boxed{}$ Children in smaller classes generally liked school much better than those in larger classes.

3 $\boxed{}$ Children in smaller classes liked mathematics more than those in larger classes.

4 $\boxed{}$ Most teachers of smaller classes did not think that their pupils had done better than those in larger classes.

5 $\boxed{}$ Teachers thought that smaller classes produced better results than larger classes.

6 $\boxed{}$ The writer thinks that even the smallest of the four classes taking part in the experiment was really a large class.

7 READING (10 marks)

Read the following paragraph about pollution. Every seventh word is missing. Write the correct word in each blank.

The Mediterranean has been described as the world's largest swimming pool. However, it can also be described now as the world's dirtiest sewer, full of rubbish, oil, chemicals and waste of all kinds. Unfortunately, most countries bordering the Mediterranean differ greatly in their attitudes to this problem. While some countries want to start ¹ _cleaning_ up the Mediterranean, others have begun ² _____ new ports to develop their oil ³ _____ and natural gas fields. Industries have now ⁴ _____ in all the countries surrounding the ⁵ _____ . It will take a century for ⁶ _____ the water in the Mediterranean to ⁷ _____ into the Atlantic Ocean and be ⁸ _____ completely by clean water. Three great ⁹ _____ , the Nile, Po and Rhone, all ¹⁰ _____ into the Mediterranean, carrying lots of ¹¹ _____ into the sea and making it very dangerous for everyone who swims in the Mediterranean and who eats fish caught there.

COMPUTERS

1 GRAMMAR RECOGNITION (10 marks)

Read the following passage. Put a circle round the letter of the correct word or words to use in each blank.

Have you ever followed instructions for knitting something or have you read a piece of music? If you have, you have behaved in a similar way ^{1}____ a computer. A computer obeys a programme to carry out a particular task. Just ^{2}____ a knitting pattern is expressed in numbers and a piece of music in lines and dots, ^{3}____ a computer programme is expressed in the form of *programming language*. ^{4}____ the English language (or any other language), there are rules of grammar, and a programme must be correct in every way.

There are hundreds of programming languages, ^{5}____ only a few are well-known and widely used. The most popular language ^{6}____ is used in offices and factories is called *Cobol*. This language is used for printing payrolls and keeping records of goods. Engineers and scientists use *Fortran* in order to carry out calculations. ^{7}____, neither of these two programmes is very popular with people working on home computers. *Basic* is the most popular language for home computers, chiefly ^{8}____ it is easy to learn and use.

^{9}____ these languages are useful for many purposes, it is time that a new simple programme was devised. ^{10}____ a programme should be not only easy to use ^{11}____ also completely reliable.

1 A to   B as   C so   D from
2 A like   B by   C so   D as
3 A so   B as   C thus   D such
4 A So   B Like   C Same   D By
5 A and   B but   C or   D if
6 A which   B where   C it   D what
7 A In addition   B Therefore   C Consequently   D However
8 A if   B so   C because   D although
9 A Because   B Although   C When   D For
10 A So   B Such   C Like   D As
11 A and   B or   C nor   D but

2 GRAMMAR PRODUCTION (10 marks)

Read the following paragraph about a computer error. One word has been omitted from each line. Put an oblique stroke (/) where the word has been omitted and write the missing word in each blank.

A few years/the Americans sent a spacecraft	1	_ago_
to examine Venus. However, it was near	2	
Venus, it necessary to alter its direction	3	
slightly by means of a computer. They tried do	4	
this typing the Fortran statement: **DO 3 1=1.3.**	5	
Unfortunately, this statement was incorrect there	6	
was a comma of a full stop. The correct statement	7	
would have sent spacecraft very close to	8	
Venus, the incorrect statement sent the spacecraft	9	
into outer space. Several billion dollars wasted	10	
as a result of such mistake.	11	

3 VOCABULARY (10 marks)

Look at the diagram and write the correct word in each blank in the passage below.

The drawing above shows a ¹_computer_ which has a ²_____ similar to that of a typewriter. It is possible to give the computer commands by means of the ³_____ keys above the letter keys. The machine has a ⁴_____ at the back so that you can connect it to a ⁵_____ , which has a ⁶_____ like a television. In the drawing below you can see a ⁷_____ which someone has written. All the information is stored on ⁸_____ , and at the side of the computer there is a ⁹_____ . A ¹⁰_____ is used to copy the information on to paper. The object like a car gear is useful for playing games on a computer and is called a ¹¹_____ .

4 READING (10 marks)

Read the following passage comparing the history of printing with that of computing. Every fourteenth word is missing. Write the correct word in each blank.

Computing is now at the same stage as printing was when the first printing presses were used. Before printing presses were invited, only rich people like kings and dukes could

1 _afford_ to buy books. Often these people were unable to read and hadn't enough 2_____ to learn. In any case, the books were so big that it was 3_____ for anyone to relax with a book as we do today. They wanted

4_____ because they were expensive and there was something magical about them. Only a 5_____ people were able to write, and it took an extremely long time to

6_____ a book. Monks and other people who could write said ordinary people could 7_____ learn to read.

   The position with computers is very similar today. A few

8_____ ago, computers were very large and expensive. Business managers and rich people ordered 9_____ but they didn't know how to use them. In many countries, however, the 10_____ has now completely changed. Lots of people not only own microcomputers but also

11_____ how to use them.

5 READING (10 marks)

Read the following reports on new computers and then complete the table below the reports. Put the most suitable figures or symbol in each space in the table.

The Altron CP802 has a large memory (512K) and a disk drive instead of the cassette recorder on the CP801 model. Although the CP801 was not difficult to use, the CP802 is even easier. Unfortunately, however, the keyboard, a weak feature of the earlier model, has not been improved, and the screen display on the colour monitor (supplied with the CP802) is of average quality. Priced at £680, the Altron CP802 is good value for money. A good instruction manual accompanies it.

The Commander 78 (£294 inclusive of special cassette recorder) has only a small memory (64K). However, the keyboard is excellent, and there is a lot of software available, especially games. The instruction manual could be slightly clearer although most people will be able to follow it with some effort. Moreover, the Commander 78 itself is simple to use. Average quality screen display.

The DDZ Micro appeared in the shops at the end of last year and is sold for exactly half the price of the Altron CP802. This model has a bigger memory than the Commander 78, although most users will not be happy until it has at least a 512K memory. A poor manual – hard to understand. Two disk drives are still necessary if you want to run complicated programmes. The display on the monitor (green on black) is very clear indeed. One weakness, however, is the length of time necessary in order to learn how to use the machine – even for simple operations. The keyboard is fairly good. A joystick is supplied free of charge.

Though rather expensive at £930, the Bright LT802 is the only computer to come with a printer in addition to the built-in colour monitor, the two disk drives and ten sample disks. Unfortunately, the screen display on the monitor tends to make your eyes ache if you look at it for long. However, the keyboard has a good, professional feel to it. Although not as easy to use as some computers, the Bright LT802 is nowhere near so difficult as the DDZ. Moreover, a well-written manual will help you to find your way around the computer. With 512K, it is good value for money.

	Altron CP802	Commander 78	DDZ Micro	Bright LT802
Ease of use	1 √√	√√	2 ___	√
Memory	X	X	3 ___	X
Screen display	√	4 ___	5 ___	6 ___
Keyboard	7 ___	√√	√	8 ___
Instructions	√√	9 ___	X	10 ___
Price	£680	£294	11 ___	£930

Key to ratings: √√   √   X
                  Good   Average   Poor

TEST 10

DISASTERS

1 GRAMMAR RECOGNITION (10 marks)

Read the following newspaper article. Put a circle round the letter of the correct word or words to use in each blank.

School tornado horror

Most of the people in Saragosa ¹___ a children's graduation ceremony in the village school when one of the worst tornadoes in American history suddenly ²___.

A sudden loud whistling sound made everyone sit up as the youngest child ³___ hands with the village mayor.

It ⁴___ to be a time of great happiness. Instead it ⁵___ in tragedy.

The children ⁶___ their certificates when the tornado hit the village without any warning.

The walls of the school building ⁷___ while most of the parents were watching the ceremony.

Tons of concrete ⁸___ crashing down on them.

Other parents ⁹___ a huge meal in the school kitchen at the time of the disaster. Afterwards no building in Saragosa remained standing. Out of a population of 185, at least 25 were dead and a further 112 were injured.

'The whole village ¹⁰___,' said police officer Paul Deishler.

'There's nothing at all here now. It ¹¹___ worse than a war zone.

1   A attend   B are attending   C were attending   D attended
2   A strikes   B is striking   C was striking   D struck
3   A has shaken   B is shaking   C shakes   D was shaking
4   A supposed   B was supposing   C was supposed   D supposing
5   A ended   B will end   C ends   D was ending
6   A were receiving   B received   C have received   D receive
7   A could fall in   B fell in   C have fallen in   D will fall in
8   A sent   B have sent   C are sent   D were sent
9   A prepared   B were preparing   C have prepared   D were prepared
10 A was going   B has gone   C will go   D is going
11 A looks   B has looked   C looked   D was looking

2 GRAMMAR PRODUCTION (10 marks)

Read the following letter and then make suitable changes to it, using the verbs in bold type. Write your answers in the blanks.

Dear Winnie,

Thank you for your letter which I received this morning. You asked me what we (¹*do*) ___were___ ___doing___ when the landslide occurred. I (²*not remember*) _____ things too clearly now but I think I (³*watch*) _____ TV and my sister (⁴*do*) _____ her homework at the time. Suddenly all the lights (⁵*go out*)_____ _____and I (⁶*frighten*) _____. I (⁷*remember*) _____ _____(⁸*call out*) _____to my parents. who (⁹*talk*)_____ _____ quietly in the next room. The next minute we (¹⁰*hear*) _____ a loud noise and the whole building (¹¹*begin*) _____ to shake.

It was a terrible experience and I never want to go through anything like it again. We are all safe now but we were very lucky.

Love, Anna

3 VOCABULARY (10 marks)

Read the sentences below very carefully. Then match each sentence with the disaster it describes. Write the numbers in the boxes below.

1 Several people were walking along when suddenly tons of earth came crashing down the hillside and blocked the road in front of them.
2 Over 50,000 people in Ethiopia have died of starvation in the past month. Questions are being asked concerning the delay in the supplies of rice and grain which were recently sent to them.
3 The winds have already strengthened considerably and the sea is now very rough indeed. As a result, ferries across the harbour have stopped sailing and all large ships have put out to sea.
4 The river overflowed in several places and huge areas of farming land are now several feet under water. Boats are being used to rescue people in nearby villages.
5 Suddenly the ground shook beneath our feet and the tall building opposite the college began to sway. Windows and doors rattled, and several bookcases in the college library came crashing down.
6 Tankers full of water were sent, but it was too late to save many of the animals and crops there. The whole area was like a vast desert.
7 Smoke poured out of the crater but no one expected an eruption. A week later, however, red hot lava began to flow down the side of the mountain.
8 It swept onwards, covering everything in its path. The travellers had to get off their camels and lie down until it had eventually passed.
9 Flames swept through the block of offices, burning everything inside. Two hours later only the empty shell of the building remained.
10 The first sign of illness was a pain in the chest, followed by a great thirst and a burning fever. Few medical supplies reached the area and consequently almost all the victims died.
11 It must have been at least twenty feet high as it swept towards the shore. In a few seconds it destroyed all the houses in its way, drowning everyone inside.

A [9] Fire B [ ] Typhoon C [ ] Earthquake D [ ] Tidal wave E [ ] Plague F [ ] Volcano
G [ ] Drought H [ ] Sandstorm I [ ] Landslide J [ ] Flood K [ ] Famine

4 READING (10 marks)

Read the following newspaper report about one of the worst earthquakes to occur in China. Write the correct word in each blank.

Beijing, Thursday

China said today that there was heavy loss of ¹ _____life_____ in the earthquake which struck Tangshan city yesterday. Survivors said that Tangshan, an industrial city of one million people 160 kilometres east of Peking, was completely ² _____.

Observers living in Beijing said it appeared that only a small part of the one million inhabitants escaped ³ _____ or injury.

Many of the men of Tangshan were working in the ⁴ _____ deep under the earth's surface when the ⁵ _____ occurred. Unfortunately, few of these miners have ⁶ _____.

A lot of people were also working in the city's ⁷ _____. Regrettably, most were ⁸ _____ under falling concrete when the buildings ⁹ _____.

The Chinese authorities have not yet given any information about the actual ¹⁰ _____ of casualties, but it is thought that tens of thousands of people have been killed. Hardly a ¹¹ _____ has been left standing.

5 READING (10 marks)

Read the following extract from a booklet. Write true (T) or false (F) for each of the sentences below, according to the information given. If the information is not in the extract, put a question mark (?).

Hungry for Change is part of a growing movement of people who want to stop famine throughout the world.
- They want to make certain that people in famine areas can protect themselves from the effects of future droughts.
- They want to make certain that enough help is quickly available for emergencies in all parts of the world.

Hungry for Change has helped to raise millions of pounds for famine relief. It has attracted a great deal of newspaper publicity for its relief work. It has also been successful in persuading the government in Britain to increase its aid budget by several million pounds and to carry out new research into improved crops.

While Hungry for Change works in Britain for an end to poverty and famine in the world, Oxfam is helping to overcome the horrors of famine in such countries as Ethiopia and Sudan with long-term development projects.

- In North West Darfur, Sudan, Oxfam is helping to increase food production.
  – **£40 buys a donkey plough.**
- In Nile Province, Sudan, Oxfam is planting trees in order to provide fuel and shelter, and to protect the soil. It is a remote area, where rainfall is poor and conditions for agriculture and forestry are difficult.
  – **It costs £2.50 to plant a tree.**
- In Arba Minch, Ethiopia, Oxfam is supporting a project to supply clean water to villages. Clean water reduces the risk of disease, especially among children.
  – **£150 protects a spring; £500 buys a pump for a well.**

1 ☑T **Hungry for Change** wants to get people to help themselves in preventing famine when there is a future shortage of water.

2 ☐ It also wants to make sure that help can be provided very quickly for people throughout the world in time of disaster.

3 ☐ Although **Hungry for Change** has collected money to help people, it wants to make sure the money is used as soon as possible.

4 ☐ Unfortunately, it has not succeeded in encouraging the British government to conduct research to help agriculture.

5 ☐ As a result of its influence, the British government is now spending more money on helping people in disaster areas.

6 ☐ The British government is carrying out research into ways of improving food production.

7 ☐ **Hungry for Change** is concerned chiefly with famine in Britain.

8 ☐ **Oxfam** plans to improve agriculture in Sudan in a very short time.

9 ☐ Until **Oxfam** began to help, there was no clean water at all in most villages in Ethiopia.

10 ☐ Donkey ploughs are wanted to increase crops in Sudan.

11 ☐ Planting trees will help indirectly to improve food production in Nile Province.

INVENTIONS

1 GRAMMAR RECOGNITION (10 marks)

Read the following sentences about the invention and development of printing. Each sentence is divided into four parts: A, B, C and D. One of these parts contains a mistake. Put a circle round the letter of the part in which there is a mistake.

1 Metal type / which could moved / was first produced/ in Korea.
   A   (B)   C   D

2 However, the first modern type /of printing press / was invented /
               A   B   C
with a German, Johannes Gutenberg, in 1439.
               D

3 The first important book /which was printing / by Gutenberg / was published in 1456.
        A   B   C   D

4 It is still / one / of most beautiful books / ever produced.
   A   B   C   D

5 It is not known / how the movable type/ used in the printing press / was making by Gutenberg.
     A   B   C   D

6 However, for several centuries /no real changes made / in the basic methods   / used for printing.
           A   B   C   D

7 Metal type was set / with hand / into pages / known as formes.
      A   B   C   D

8 These pages / were inked/ and printed / on to single sheets by paper.
   A   B   C   D

9 The first / self-inking press / was built / to Stephen Ruggles in 1839.
   A   B   C   D

10 Methods of printing / have developed / by the newspaper industry / over the past hundred years.
      A   B   C   D

11 Modern high-speed printing /   carried out on a rotary press, / using continuous paper /
          A   B   C
from a huge roll.
     D

2 GRAMMAR PRODUCTION (10 marks)

Read the following paragraph about a computer error. One word is missing from each line. Put an oblique stroke (/) where the word has been omitted and write the missing word in each blank.

Nowadays a lot of important inventions/carried   1 ___*are*___

out scientists working for large industrial firms.   2 _____

However, there are still opportunities other people   3 _____

to invent various things. In Britain, is a weekly   4 _____

television programme attempts to show   5 _____

all various devices which people have recently   6 _____

invented. The people organising programme   7 _____

receive information about 700 inventions year.   8 _____

New ideas can still be developed private inventors.   9 _____

However, is important to consider these questions: 10 _____

Will it work? Will it wanted? Is it new?   11 _____

3 VOCABULARY (5 marks)

Complete the following paragraph by writing the correct word in each blank. The first three letters in each word are given and the meaning of each word is given (in order) below the paragraph.

Although the Chinese were responsible for the [1]inv_*ention*___ of such important things as

gunpowder, the compass, paper-making and silk [2]man_____ , the ancient Greeks were also

very [3]ing_____ and invented all kinds of useful [4]dev_____ . Heron, for example,

[5]des_____ the world's first steam engine although it was never put to any

[6]pra_____ use.

1   production of something (especially new or useful) for the first time
2   method of producing something (in large quantities) by machinery
3   clever at making or inventing things
4   a tool, machine, or instrument which has been cleverly thought out.
5   drew the plans for
6   concerned with action, practice, or actual conditions rather than ideas

4 VOCABULARY (5 marks)

Write the correct word in each blank. A dash (—) is shown for each missing letter and every other letter is given in each word.

Many people think inventors suddenly have an idea which results in a [1]r_e_v_o_l_u_t_i_o_n_a_r_y invention. This is not usually the case. Inventors certainly need to have [2]o__i__i__a__ ideas but most inventions are the result of hard work in the [3]l__b__r__t__r__ and careful [4]e__p__r__m__n__s by experts. Each invention is then put through all kinds of [5]t__s__s before eventually a [6]p__t__n__ and licence to manufacture are granted.

5 READING (10 marks)

Read the following passage about the invention of a device for getting rid of cockroaches. Every seventh word is missing. Write the correct word in each blank.

Singapore housewife invents useful device

A useful device for getting rid of cockroaches has just been invented by a housewife. The device is called 'Stop-Roach' and [1]_____will_____ soon be on sale in department [2]_____ and large shops.

  'Stop-Roach' consists of [3]_____ hollow cylinder and movable valve. It [4]_____ placed in any drain or opening [5]_____ there are cockroaches. Cockroaches trying to [6]_____ the house through the drain will [7]_____ it impossible to get through the [8]_____ .

  'Stop-Roach' has been subjected to thorough [9]_____ by the Environment Ministry and the [10]_____ has now been patented. It has [11]_____ found completely foolproof against invasions of cockroaches from drains and sewers.

  It is expected that 'Stop-Roach' will be on sale very soon for under ten dollars.

6 READING (5 marks)

Read the paragraph about the invention of the phonograph, the first recording machine.

The phonograph was invented in 1877 by Thomas Edison. It consisted of a brass cylinder which was mounted on a heavy wooden base. A sheet of tinfoil was wrapped over grooves cut on the brass cylinder. A funnel which was shaped like a cone was used to focus sound on to a metal diaphragm. This diaphragm touched a steel stylus containing a sharp tip which pressed on the sheet of tinfoil. When the brass cylinder was turned by means of the handle at one end, the stylus pressed into the foil over one of the grooves and thus recorded the sound. A large flywheel on one end of the cylinder helped to keep the speed steady. The cylinder was then wound back to its original position. When the handle at the other end was turned again, the cylinder revolved and the original sound was reproduced.

Now label the diagram below.

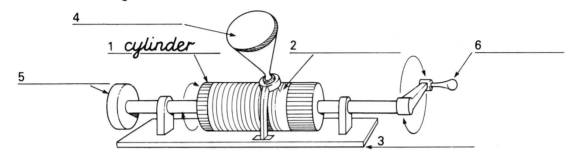

7 READING (5 marks)

Read the following passage about the invention of a new kind of armchair. Write true (T) or false (F) for each of the sentences below, according to the information given. If the information is not given, put a question mark (?).

A lot of people like to play their records as loudly as possible. The result is that the rest of the family and the neighbours often complain if they don't like the music. One answer to this problem is to wear headphones, but headphones are usually uncomfortable.

An armchair which has a record-player system built into it has just been designed by a British engineer, Stephen Court.

The armchair looks like an ordinary armchair with a high back. However, each of the two sides of the chair has three loudspeakers inside to reproduce middle and high sounds. Low sounds are reproduced by a pair of loudspeakers in a hollow space under the seat. Anyone who sits in the chair hears sounds coming from all round his/her head.

Because we cannot tell the exact source from which low sounds come, it doesn't matter that they come from underneath or behind. It is the higher sounds coming from the sides of the chair that create a stereo effect.

These sounds travel only a few inches to reach the listener's ears. Consequently, it takes only a little power to make the music sound very loud. Only a small amount of sound leaks out from behind the chair into the room to disturb others. Most of the sound is absorbed by the listener.

1 [T] Stephen Court has just invented an armchair which can play music.

2 [ ] The armchair has very comfortable headphones attached to it.

3 [ ] The armchair is like an ordinary armchair but it contains speakers in both its sides and underneath the part where someone sits.

4 [ ] Most people can tell exactly the direction from where low sounds are coming.

5 [ ] Most people nowadays prefer listening to sound which comes from more than one speaker even if the quality is not too good.

6 [ ] People sitting in chairs near the armchair will not be able to hear most of the sound.

HABITS AND CUSTOMS

1 GRAMMAR RECOGNITION (10 marks)

Read the following conversation about the increase of traffic in a city. Put a circle round the letter of the correct word or words to use in each blank.

A   The traffic ^{1}____ much worse now.

B   Yes, it ^{2}____ easy to park in the city centre.

A   That's right, but not any longer. ^{3}____ more and more difficult in the past few years.

B   I remember when you ^{4}____ outside any shop you ^{5}____ .

A   Yes, you ^{6}____ anywhere at all at one time, but now there are parking meters everywhere.

B   And they ^{7}____ so many of the roads into one-way streets now.

A   I know. There have already been one or two nasty accidents. People ^{8}____ the new system yet.

B   It'll take a while before everyone ^{9}____ familiar with it.

A   Actually, I miss the good old days when we ^{10}____ to the shops. There were no cars at all on the roads then.

B   Mind you, I must say ^{11}____ travelling by car!

  1 A got   B is getting   C used to get   D getting
  2 A would be   B used to be   C is being   D has been
  3 A It's got   B It gets   C It used to get   D It was getting
  4 A can be parking   B could park   C can park   D could be parking
  5 A go to   B are going to   C have gone to   D were going to
  6 A could park   B can park   C are able to park   D could be parking
  7 A turned   B have turned   C turn   D used to turn
  8 A used to   B using to   C aren't used to   D aren't using to
  9 A has become   B shall become   C could become   D is becoming
10 A cycle   B have cycled   C are used to cycling   D used to cycle
11 A I'd prefer   B I prefer   C I'm preferring   D I was preferring

2 GRAMMAR PRODUCTION (10 marks)

Use *used to* to change each of the verbs in bold type but only where possible. If you cannot change it, copy the verb as it is. Write each verb in the appropriate blank.

Long ago there (¹**was**) ___*used to be*___ a beautiful island in the Atlantic Ocean. The island,

(²**called**) ___*called*___ Atlantis, (³**was surrounded**) _____ by nine rings of

land and nine rings of water. All kinds of fruit (⁴**grew**) _____ on Atlantis, and the

island also (⁵**had**) _____ lots of precious metals. The people of Atlantis (⁶**built**)

_____ a large empire and (⁷**traded**) _____ with many countries.

According to the Greeks, Atlantis (⁸**lay**) _____ beyond Gibraltar and (⁹**was**

swallowed up) _____ in the sea. However, many now (¹⁰**think**)

_____ Atlantis was the island of Thera. As a result of a volcanic eruption, Thera

(¹¹**sank**) _____ into the sea and its advanced civilisation suddenly

(¹²**disappeared**) _____ .

3 VOCABULARY (5 marks)

Complete the following paragraph by writing the correct word in each blank. A dash (—) is shown for each missing letter and every other letter is given in each word. The meaning of each word is given (in order) below the paragraph.

Many people find it difficult to learn the ¹c_u_s_t_o_m_s of another country when they go abroad.

Each country observes its own special ²t—a—i—i—n— and ³f—s—i—a—s just as

individuals have their own ⁴h—b—t— and daily ⁵r—u—i—e—. In Britain, for example, it is not

the usual ⁶p—a—t—c— for shops to stay open after 6 pm, as in many other countries.

1   things that people in a country or group always do in certain circumstances
2   customs which people in a group have observed for a long time
3   days, etc. when people usually have holidays to celebrate special events
4   things that people do regularly or frequently
5   ways of doing a regular set of jobs in a fixed order
6   normal way of doing something

4 VOCABULARY (5 marks)

Read the following sentences. Put a circle round the letter of the correct word to use in each blank.

1   You'll probably see Dave on the 4.30 bus; he _____ catches it to school.
    A sometimes   **B** traditionally   **C** routinely   (**D**) usually

2   The doctor told me to take the pills _____ three times a day.
    A invariably   **B** regularly   **C** customarily   **D** frequently

3   Timothy is _____ late when he meets Mabel.
    A frequently   **B** routinely   **C** customarily   **D** practically

4   People who _____ tell lies should be punished severely.
    A traditionally   **B** habitually   **C** practically   **D** customarily

5   Would you believe it! It _____ rains for this particular festival!
    A inconsistently   **B** customarily   **C** invariably   **D** changelessly

6   Linda _____ scores very high marks in grammar tests but quite low marks in composition writing.
    A traditionally   **B** consistently   **C** customarily   **D** routinely

5 READING (10 marks)

Read the following descriptions of hats which some men in Britain wear, or used to wear.

Bowler: A bowler hat was first worn by an English landowner in 1849 to protect his head from the low branches of trees while he was shooting birds. He ordered the hat from a shop in London and tested it by putting it on the floor and stamping on it twice. The hat was undamaged, and the landowner immediately bought it. Soon this type of hat became very popular. It is completely round at the top and has only a narrow brim. Most office-workers in London used to wear bowlers until a few years ago.

Cap: This type of hat used to be worn by workers in Britain. It was especially popular during the first half of this century but is no longer worn as much. It is made of soft cloth and is quite flat with a peak which extends for two or three inches over the forehead.

Beret: This is similar in certain ways to a cap, but it is worn chiefly by soldiers. It is flat and completely circular in shape, and it has no peak.

Fez: This hat used to be worn by a lot of men in the Middle East. It has a tassel and it is shaped like a cone with a flat top.

Trilby: In 1894 the actors in a play by George du Maurier wore soft felt hats with wide brims. The top of this type of hat is dented.

Topper: This is a tall hat with a fairly narrow brim. It is cylindrical in shape and has a flat, circular top. When someone first wore it in London in 1797, people gathered round and women fainted. It soon became very popular and people used to wear it for weddings and other formal occasions. Even now it is worn for these occasions.

Write the correct name under each hat.

| 1 | 2 | 3 | 4 | 5 | 6 |

trilby _____ _____ _____ _____ _____ _____

Write true (T) or false (F) for each of the sentences below, according to the information given. If no information is given, put a question mark (?).

1 [T] A lot of clerks in London used to wear bowlers until recently.

2 [ ] A bowler is quite a soft hat.

3 [ ] Although caps were worn a lot, only older people wear them now.

4 [ ] A fez is exactly the same shape as a pyramid.

5 [ ] The top of a trilby is completely flat and circular.

6 [ ] People were very surprised to see the first topper.

6 READING (10 marks)

Read the following passage about the Ancient Mexicans, their customs and religious beliefs. Write the correct word in each blank.

The Ancient Mexicans used to respect and fear the sun. They were frightened that the sun might stop rising. As a result, they used to make sacrifices so that the sun god would continue to give them day and [1] *night* and the four seasons.

Farmers, however, used to worship the rain [2]_____ almost as much as the [3]_____ god. Even today there are ruins of great pyramids they used to [4]_____ to worship the sun and the rain gods.

Another popular god was the wind god, which took the form of a [5]_____ with feathers. This feathered snake was also the god of knowledge for the Ancient Mexicans. Under its influence, civilisation [6]_____ throughout Mexico, which at that time was mostly a peaceful [7]_____ with plenty of skilled craftsmen and traders. Unfortunately, news of this [8]_____ eventually spread, and Mexico was invaded from the far north. Later, other people called Aztecs settled in Mexico. At first they used to [9]_____ on an island in a lake where Mexico City now is. The [10]_____ used to grow maize and they built beautiful towns and temples, developing [11]_____ into one of the most advanced civilisations of the time.

TEST 13

COMMERCE AND INDUSTRY

1 GRAMMAR RECOGNITION (10 marks)

Read the following article. Put a circle round the letter of the correct word or words to use in each blank.

The man who made and lost a fortune ¹___ kitchen furniture is back in business again. 37-year-old Timothy Lindlaw is now designing ²___ for offices – from the director's suite to the secretarial office.

Lindlaw had always had a lot of good ideas. After he ³___ a highly successful computer business for two years, he started his second business in a small garage, selling and installing kitchen furniture. He ⁴___ his first million pounds by the time he was thirty. Then he went on to earn over five million in three years.

But, after ⁵___ with the managers of his company, he suddenly dismissed them.

Within six months the business had gone bankrupt. And so ⁶___ Lindlaw. 'I had made five million pounds before things ⁷___ to go wrong,' he said. 'I was just unlucky to lose it later. All companies ⁸___ through good times – and through bad times. Now ⁹___ several lessons which I'll never forget.'

He said that he ¹⁰___ to call his new company 'Office-Fit' and was already very successful.

Lindlaw said that it was a market worth hundreds of millions. He added that, until he started, no one ¹¹___ of designing and supplying furniture for whole business companies, according to their individual requirements.

1 A manufacture   (B) manufacturing   C to manufacture   D manufactured
2 A furniture   B furnitures   C some furnitures   D a furniture
3 A has run   B runs   C was running   D had run
4 A has made   B used to make   C had made   D would make
5 A quarrel   B quarrelling   C quarrelled   D have quarrelled
6 A has   B does   C did   D had
7 A have begun   B began   C begin   D would begin
8 A went   B have gone   C had gone   D go
9 A I learn   B I've learnt   C I learnt   D I'd learnt
10 A had decided   B was deciding   C decided   D has decided
11 A had ever thought   B ever thinks   C would ever think   D has ever thought

2 GRAMMAR PRODUCTION (10 marks)

Read the following sales report. One word is missing from each line. Put an oblique stroke (/) where the word has been omitted and write the missing word in each blank.

Report to Sales Manager

The period January 1st to April 30th has/one of intense	1	*been*
activity, the sales figures being much higher than been	2	_____
forecast (24.5 per cent). Previously it had expected	3	_____
that sales be approximately the same as those from	4	_____
October December of last year. Some members of the	5	_____
board of directors had actually forecast small loss.	6	_____
Much of the increase in sales can attributed to better	7	_____
advertising. Moreover, sales force was increased.	8	_____
Most successful sales of exercise books and art paper.	9	_____
The market for such products computer accessories,	10	_____
however, was disappointing, contrary to what been	11	_____

originally expected.

3 VOCABULARY (5 marks)

Read the following paragraph showing the responsibilities of a general manager in a particular company. Then select the correct word which can be used to replace the words in *italics*. Write the number in the correct box below.

A general manager is responsible for [1]*organising everything so that people work together effectively.* This involves [2]*the products (or services) which are sold,* [3]*obtaining the materials for making these products,* [4]*the company's accounts,* [5]*his staff or work force, their welfare, promotion, etc.;* and [6]*helping everyone outside the company to have a good opinion of the company.*

A ☐ personnel   C ☐ sales   E ☐ public relations

B ☐ finance   D [1] coordination F ☐ supply

4 VOCABULARY (5 marks)

Look at the following graph and read the sales report below it. Put a circle round the letter of the correct word or words to use in each blank.

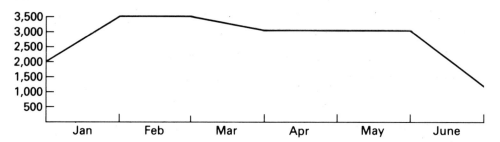

At the beginning of the year sales ^{1}_____ at 2,000 personal computers. Sales then climbed steadily and reached a ^{2}_____ of 3,500 personal computers in February but fell slightly to 3,100 at the end of March and ^{3}_____ during the next two months. By the end of June, however, sales had fallen ^{4}_____ to 1,400 (an all-time ^{5}_____). The ^{6}_____ number of personal computers sold during the first six months was thus 2,700 per month.

1 **A** sat **B** raced **C** marched **D** stood
2 **A** height **B** top **C** peak **D** summit
3 **A** levelled off **B** smoothed out **C** straightened out **D** ruled off
4 **A** dramatically **B** playfully **C** theatrically **D** tragically
5 **A** bottom **B** depth **C** hole **D** low
6 **A** medium **B** average **C** middle **D** central

5 READING (10 marks)

Read the paragraphs below about car sales in Britain. Write the correct word in each blank.

The demand for new cars ^{1}__*beat*__ all records last month. Sales topped 400,000 for the first time figures showed yesterday. In the first twenty days of the month 327,000 cars had been ^{2}_____

The figures showed that the ^{3}_____ for new cars had been even ^{4}_____ than that during the previous month. Total ^{5}_____ this year are so far fifteen per cent above the corresponding figure for last year.

Until last month, Ranger cars had sold only 58,370 cars so far this year – a drop of nearly 9,000 on the same period last ^{6}_____. However, with the ^{7}_____ in sales last month, the total

8_____ of Ranger cars sold this year is now 93,280. While car sales have increased generally, the

sale of imported cars is 9_____ sharply from sixty per cent to fifty-two per cent this year.

   The biggest increase in the share of the market has been achieved by Peret-Alpine cars, whose sales

10_____ by thirty per cent last month. This success has resulted in increased employment in

Tanningley; at least 120 new 11_____ have been created.

6 READING (10 marks)

Read the following sentences carefully. Then use the information in the sentences to complete the graph (similar to the graph in Question 4 opposite). You will be awarded two marks for **each** correct section.

1   A total of 200,000 cars were exported from Narawa in 1980. As a result of two new factories, this number had doubled by the end of 1982.

2   In the following year, however, several strikes and a serious oil shortage, hit the car industry in Narawa very badly. Consequently, the number of cars exported fell by 100,000.

3   However, when labour relations improved in 1984 and there was an increase in the supply of oil, there was a dramatic rise that year to 600,000.

4   This number fluctuated between 550,000 and 600,000 during the following two years.

5   Then, in 1987, a slight upward trend was followed by a marked rise by the middle of 1988, when the number of cars exported exceeded 800,000.

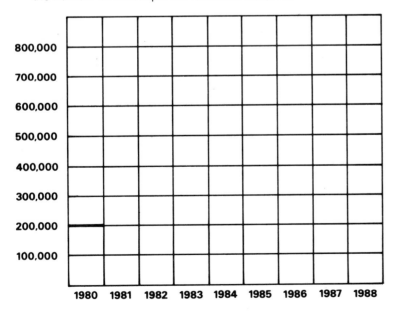

TEST 14

ENERGY

1 GRAMMAR RECOGNITION (10 marks)

Read the following paragraph. Put a circle round the letter of the correct word or words to use in each blank.

When man first learned how to make a fire, he began to use fuel for the first time. The first fuel he used was probably wood. As time ¹____ , man eventually discovered that substances such as coal and oil ²____ .

Coal ³____ very widely as a source of energy until the last century. With the coming of the industrial revolution, it was soon realised that production ⁴____ if coal was used instead of wood. Nowadays, many of the huge factories and electricity generating stations ⁵____ to function if there was no coal.

In the last twenty or thirty years, however, the use of coal ⁶____ . As a result, there have been changes in the coal industry. It ⁷____ that more people ⁸____ coal if oil and gas were not so readily available.

There is more than enough coal in the world for man's needs for the next two hundred years if our use of coal ⁹____ . Unfortunately, however, about half of the world's coal ¹⁰____ . Mining much of it ¹¹____ very expensive even if it was possible to use new equipment.

1 A passes   B used to pass   C would pass   (D) passed
2 A are burning   B would burn   C have burnt   D were burnt
3 A not used   B did not use   C not using   D was not used
4 A doubles   B had doubled   C will double   D would double
5 A were unable   B would be unable   C will be unable   D are unable
6 A has declined   B will decline   C declines   D would decline
7 A believed   B is believing   C believing   D is believed
8 A would use   B used   C use   D will use
9 A did not increase   B would not increase   C does not increase   D may not increase
10 A would never use   B may never be used   C would never be used   D may never use
11 A was   B used to be   C would be   D has been

2 GRAMMAR PRODUCTION (10 marks)

Read the following paragraph about oil and gas supplies. One word is missing from each line. Put an oblique stroke (/) where the word has been omitted and write the missing word in each blank.

Although the world's energy resources/taken many	1	*have*
millions of years to produce, we quickly beginning	2	_____
to exhaust these supplies. Recently UN committee	3	_____
reported that world's oil and gas supplies	4	_____
would about 100 years if used carefully. The report	5	_____
stated that there be enough oil and gas for a century	6	_____
only if the present demand could controlled. If the	7	_____
demand continued grow, the report said that fuel	8	_____
supplies last for less than forty years. According	9	_____
to the report, governments now take steps to	10	_____
control the amounts of fossil fuels are used.	11	_____

3 VOCABULARY (10 marks)

Put a circle round the letter of the best word to use in each blank.

There is now increasing concern about the world's energy ^{1}____ , particularly about those involving fossil ^{2}____ . In less than a hundred years we shall probably ^{3}____ all the present ^{4}____ of oil and gas. The world's coal ^{5}____ should last longer but, once used, these cannot be ^{6}____ . It is important, therefore, that we should develop such ^{7}____ sources of energy as solar energy and nuclear energy as well as water and wind ^{8}____ (classed as ^{9}____ energy). Until these energy ^{10}____ are widely used, it is important for the developed countries to reduce energy ^{11}____ as much as possible.

1 A possessions   (B) resources   C goods   D materials
2 A fuels   B powers   C forms   D energies
3 A end   B complete   C total   D exhaust
4 A findings   B productions   C amounts   D sources
5 A reserves   B stores   C mines   D contents
6 A updated   B repeated   C renewed   D produced
7 A traditional   B alternative   C revolutionary   D surprising
8 A force   B strength   C power   D motion
9 A repeatable   B continual   C renewable   D continuous
10 A goods   B supplies   C provisions   D materials
11 A exhaustion   B destruction   C waste   D consumption

4 READING (10 marks)

Read the following sentences about the different forms of energy available. Match the sentences in Part One with the correct sentences in Part Two and write the correct letter in each box.

Part One

1 $\boxed{H}$ Muscles and wood were the first sources of energy used by early man.

2 ☐ Coal made the Industrial Revolution in the nineteenth century possible.

3 ☐ Today we depend on oil more than any other fuel.

4 ☐ Gas is considered as a 'mineral' because, together with coal, it is part of the earth's crust.

5 ☐ Hydroelectric power is used to produce electricity.

6 ☐ Geothermal energy is produced from the heat stored in the earth's core.

7 ☐ The wind was used as a power source over 1,300 years ago in Persia when the first windmill was built to turn a millstone.

8 ☐ Waves have enormous power.

9 ☐ Incoming tides can be trapped behind a dam across a bay or an estuary.

10 ☐ A huge amount of solar energy reaches the earth's outer atmosphere.

11 ☐ Nuclear fuels, such as uranium-235 and plutonium, can be made to produce immense heat by a process called 'fission'.

Part Two

A Like oil, it is a fossil fuel and is thus a non-renewable source of energy.

B One danger, however, is in getting rid of the radioactive wastes which are produced.

C They increase and decrease more slowly than the wind, thus making them easier to use as a source of energy.

D It was the first fossil fuel to be used to power machinery.

E However, it is thinly spread, and collecting it in countries like Britain and northern Europe is still difficult and expensive.

F It is used as fuel in cars, ships and aeroplanes, and even in rockets.

G It is produced by the fall of water trapped in a dam.

H It took thousands of years to progress to using coal on a large scale.

I   This internal heat helps to produce geysers and steam springs and can be used to generate electricity in countries like New Zealand.

J   The water is then allowed to flow out past water wheels as the tide goes out.

K   For modern purposes, however, it is necessary to build a machine which can store the energy obtained for use on calm days.

5 READING (10 marks)

Read the following paragraph about the use of solar energy. Every ninth word is missing. Write the correct word in each blank.

About twenty per cent of the world's present energy already comes from the sun in one form or another. Special devices have already been made available to ¹ *place/put* on the roofs of houses and flats to ² _____ the sun's rays and thus heat water. Thousands ³ _____ these devices are now being used to provide ⁴ _____ in homes throughout the United States while more ⁵ _____ a million solar water-heating units have already been ⁶ _____ in homes in Japan. Other purposes for which ⁷ _____ energy is at present being used include the ⁸ _____ of salt from seawater, irrigation and sewage disposal.

⁹ _____ most people in developing countries, the need is ¹⁰ _____ for air-conditioners or central heating but for cheap ¹¹ _____ of cooking food, drying crops and lighting homes.

TEST 15

ACCIDENTS

1 GRAMMAR RECOGNITION (10 marks)

Read the following sentences. Put a circle round the letter of the correct word or words to use in each blank.

A What on earth ¹____ if the brakes of your car didn't work?
   A do you do   B have you done   C will you do   (D) would you do

B I've no idea. I suppose ²____ on to the pavement to slow down.
   A I drive   B I'm driving   C I'll drive   D I'd drive

A But you couldn't do that if there ³____ people on the pavement.
   A were   B have been   C are   D would be
   If the car ⁴____ the pavement, it'd probably hit one of them.
   A mounts   B will mount   C has mounted   D mounted

B Fortunately ⁵____ to me so far. But why do you ask?
   A it never happens   B it'll never happen   C it's never happened
   D it'd never happen

A It actually happened to me this morning. I put my foot on the brakes but nothing happened. I didn't know what to do. At first I thought ⁶____ to pass the lorry in front of me.
   A I tried   B I'd try   C I'll try   D I'd tried
   But then I realised that I'd probably hit an oncoming car if ⁷____ that.
   A I did   B I'd do   C I'd done   D I do

B Good gracious. What did you do?

A Fortunately, there was a hill just a few yards ahead. It was very steep and it slowed me down. If the hill hadn't been there, I ⁸____ here now talking to you!
   A wouldn't be   B hadn't been   C shan't be   D wasn't

B If I ⁹____ you, I'd sell that car.
   A was   B would be   C have been   D were

A I'm having the car completely checked.

B If ¹⁰____ to me, you wouldn't have bought the car in the first place.
   A you listen   B you've listened   C you'd listen   D you'd listened

A Maybe not, but if I hadn't bought this car, ¹¹____ another old car with something equally wrong with it.
   A I'd probably buy   B I probably bought   C I'd probably have bought
   D I'd probably bought

2 GRAMMAR PRODUCTION (10 marks)

Read the following newspaper report and use a suitable form of each verb in bold type.
Write your answers in the blanks.

Several cars were involved in the pile-up because no one (¹**try**) *tried/had tried* to phone

the police for help. If someone (²**call**)_____ the police immediately, they

(³**be able**)_____ to send an ambulance and also direct the traffic, thus

(⁴**prevent**)_____ the other accidents. A passer-by (⁵**tell**)_____

police that he (⁶**decide**)_____ to free the trapped driver before

(⁷**phone**)_____ the police. He said that the trapped driver

(⁸**beg**)_____ him not to leave him. If he (⁹**go off**)_____ to look

for a phone or to seek help, the driver (¹⁰**be**)_____ in the car when it

(¹¹**hit**)_____ by the second car.

3 VOCABULARY (10 marks)

Read the following account of an accident. Put a circle round the letter of the correct word
or words to use in each blank.

There was a nasty ¹___ at Newton cross-roads yesterday morning. A bus overturned, and some of the passengers were badly ²___. Several ³___ helped to pull people out of the ⁴___ and give them ⁵___ until help arrived. Soon the injured were taken to the nearest hospital by ambulance, but there were so many that the ⁶___ department there had difficulty in treating them all. Most of the passengers were found to be suffering from severe ⁷___. The bus had crashed into a brand new car and had completely ⁸___ it, although fortunately there was no one in the car. Moreover, the new car was fully ⁹___. The police took the names and addresses of as many ¹⁰___ as possible. It is believed that the injured passengers have the right to claim ¹¹___.

1 A event   (B) accident   C happening   D emergency
2 A pained   B wounded   C knocked down   D injured
3 A bystanders   B spectators   C audience   D supporters
4 A wreckage   B crash   C damage   D accident
5 A medicine   B cures   C remedy   D first aid
6 A injury   B ambulance   C casualty   D operating
7 A surprise   B shock   C worry   D nervousness
8 A damaged   B knocked   C wrecked   D crashed
9 A insured   B guaranteed   C protected   D purchased
10 A suspects   B witnesses   C viewers   D judges
11 A rewards   B prizes   C refund   D compensation

4 READING (10 marks)

Read the following questions and answers from an insurance form. Match the questions with the appropriate answers and write the correct letter in each box.

Questions

1 [D] Where can your car be inspected during normal working hours?

2 [ ] Who do you think was responsible for the accident?

3 [ ] Would it be possible for you to take photographs of the place of the accident, showing what you could see at the time?

4 [ ] Were the police involved? If so, could you inform us of the name and number of the police officer and the police station from which he/she came?

5 [ ] Were you injured at all? If so, please give us the fullest details, even if the injuries were minor.

6 [ ] Was it necessary for you or anyone else involved in the accident to receive hospital treatment?

7 [ ] Have you fully recovered from your injuries?

8 [ ] Are the passengers in your car claiming compensation?

9 [ ] Did you lose any time off work?

10 [ ] Did you lose any earnings? If so, why did you lose them?

11 [ ] How long were you without your car and how much inconvenience did this cause?

Answers

A It was necessary for me to stay at home for three days.

B I was thrown out of the car and received cuts on my face. My right wrist was badly sprained.

C Five weeks. I had to spend approximately £60 on taxi fares and wasted considerable time in travelling to and from work by bus (having to change buses three times on each journey from my home to work).

D Eastern Export Company, 31 Seaview Road, Calton.

E My injuries were treated in the Casualty Department of Rosehurst Hospital but I was not admitted. However, my brother, who was a passenger, was admitted to hospital with back injuries and a broken arm.

F Yes, I have.

G I regret that I do not have a camera.

H My brother intends to make a claim.

I   The driver of the oncoming car. You will note from my previous accident report that he overtook a lorry on a bend.

J   Yes, PC Richard Lime. 40296. West Shenton Police Station.

K   Yes. Four days' wages were deducted from my monthly salary as a result of my inability to use my injured hand to write.

5 READING (10 marks)

Look at the following graph showing the number of accidents at the crossroads outside the village of Meanwood.

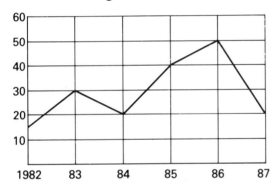

Now read the following notes describing the changes which took place at the crossroads between 1982 and 1987.

1982 Odeon Cinema built
1983 Traffic lights put up
1984 Offices opened

1985 Accident warning signs put up
1986 Pedestrian bridge built

Read the following paragraph about the number of road accidents at the crossroads outside the village of Meanwood. Write the correct figures or words in the blanks.

There were fifteen road accidents at the crossroads between 1982 and [1]_____*1983*_____

after a new [2]_____ was built. This number [3]_____

slightly the following year as a result of the introduction of [4]_____ but rose

rapidly from 1984 to 1985 as a result of some new [5]_____ . The number of

accidents reached a peak of [6]_____ during the years 1985 to 1986.

It would probably have been [7]_____ if [8]_____ hadn't been

put up. The building of a [9]_____ in [10]_____ fortunately

resulted in a [11]_____ in the number of accidents.

TEST 16

REVISION TEST

1 GRAMMAR RECOGNITION (10 marks)

Read the following paragraph. Put a circle round the letter of the correct word or words to use in each blank.

Almost a hundred thousand people ¹_____ and half a million homes destroyed as a result of an earthquake in Tokyo in 1923. The earthquake began a minute before noon when the inhabitants of Tokyo ²_____ their midday meals. Thousands of stoves were overturned as soon as the earth ³_____ to shake. As a result, small fires ⁴_____ everywhere and quickly spread. The fire engines were prevented ⁵_____ to help because many of the roads ⁶_____ open. It was impossible to use fire fighting equipment as most of the water pipes ⁷_____ . Consequently, over ninety per cent of the damage ⁸_____ by fire rather than by the collapse of buildings. Most of those ⁹_____ were not killed in the earthquake itself but in the fires which followed. If the earthquake had occurred at night while people ¹⁰_____ , far fewer ¹¹_____ .

1   A have been killed   (B) were killed   C had been killed   D would be killed
2   A cooked   B were cooking   C would cook   D had cooked
3   A began   B was beginning   C used to begin   D began
4   A were breaking out   B would break out   C have broken out   D broke out
5   A from going   B to go   C for going   D he went
6   A had cracked   B cracking   C crack   D were cracking
7   A would burst   B had burst   C have burst   D used to burst
8   A caused   B was causing   C causing   D was caused
9   A who died   B died   C they died   D dying
10 A would sleep   B have slept   C had slept   D were sleeping
11 A died   B would die   C had died   D would have died

2 GRAMMAR PRODUCTION (10 marks)

Read the following newspaper report and use a suitable form of each verb in bold type. Write your answers in the blanks.

28 HURT IN TRAIN CRASH

Twenty-eight people (¹**injure**) _were injured_ after a train which (²**carry**) _____ workers on a one-day holiday (³**hit**) _____ the buffers of Blackpool North Station yesterday.

When interviewed, British Rail (⁴**say**) _____ 'The train (⁵**travel**) _____ at only eight kilometres per hour as it (⁶**enter**) _____ the station and for some reason (⁷**fail**) _____ (⁸**stop**) _____. An inquiry (⁹**holds**) _____ as soon as possible.'

Those who (¹⁰**hurt**) _____ fortunately (¹¹**suffer**) _____ only shock and minor injuries.

3 VOCABULARY (5 marks)

Complete the following paragraph by writing the correct word in each blank. The first three letters in each word are given.

It is ¹pre_dicted_ that the price of gold will ²flu_____ during the coming year, rising and falling by about ten per cent. After last year's ³dra_____ rise in the value of gold from $1,250 an ounce to $2,700, ⁴dem_____ has now fallen slightly and the price has ⁵lev_____ off again. As a result, it is now a good time to buy gold before there is a ⁶mar_____ increase in price next year.

4 VOCABULARY (5 marks)

Read the following paragraph about the invention of computers.

The electronic computer is the most significant invention since the steam engine. While the industrial revolution previously changed the nature of manual work, the computer revolution is now changing the work done by the brain. Nowadays micro-computers are manufactured in hundreds of thousands and are constantly being equipped with more and more ingenious devices. Contrary to popular belief, computers themselves cannot make mistakes. The answer will always be correct if the programme fed into the computer is correct.

Which words in the paragraph have the following meanings? Write the correct word from the paragraph in each blank.

1   produced (in a factory) — *manufactured*

2   instruments (especially ones cleverly thought out) — _____

3   very important change in methods of working — _____

4   set of instructions to carry out something — _____

5   something made or used for the first time — _____

6   clever (involving new equipment, methods or ideas) — _____

5 READING (10 marks)

Read the following paragraph about the invention of robots. Every seventh word is missing. Write the correct word in each blank.

When robots are widely used in the home, they will probably be used to do the cleaning, table-laying, scrubbing and washing-up, but it is considered unlikely that they will be used to do the cooking – at least, not in the near future.

In factories, mobile robots are already [1] *used* to carry out a large number [2]_____ the distribution and assembly tasks while [3]_____ beings carry out research and produce [4]_____ for new products. Amongst the numerous [5]_____ on the farm, robots will drive [6]_____ , keeping their eyes on the ground [7]_____ front to guide the tractor along [8]_____ straight line.

The majority of the [9]_____ used at present do not look [10]_____ human beings at all because their [11]_____ is chiefly functional.

6 READING (10 marks: ½ each)

Read the following passage about sources of energy. Then complete the table below.

Although they are safe to use in the short term, coal, gas and oil present a long-term threat to the environment. All three types of fossil fuels produce carbon dioxide in far greater quantities than plants can use. The carbon dioxide then accumulates in the atmosphere and may even increase the earth's 'heat load' and lead to global rises in temperature. Thus, contrary to popular belief, the use of coal, gas and oil is not as safe as was originally thought. Furthermore, all three fossil fuels are non-renewable forms of energy.

Geothermal power is unlikely ever to be an energy source of major importance. It is limited and is exploitable in only a few places.

Hydro-power (in the form of waterfalls and dams) offers a much more useful source of energy. It is also renewable but its availability is limited. Dams cannot be built in certain areas. In addition, dams may have a damaging effect on a locality, resulting in the loss of farming land and the silting up of rivers. Large dams are also capable of causing changes in the world's climate.

Wind power is a pollution-free source of renewable energy but it cannot be used in many parts of the world where there is insufficient wind. It is also impossible to use wind power efficiently at present.

Wave power is a better source of energy in certain ways but it is clearly not practicable to build dams across every river estuary or to cover seas with expensive equipment. It is also ineffective where the sea is usually calm. Wave power, however, is non-polluting and does not add to the earth's heat load.

Solar power is renewable, it does not cause pollution and it does not add to the earth's heat load. Unfortunately, solar power is not distributed equally, and in northern latitudes it is difficult to collect and store. Solar power also requires expensive equipment.

Finally, nuclear power provides a very efficient and renewable power source. However, not only is there a great danger of leaks or accidents but there is also the problem of the disposal of radioactive waste.

	R	Pol	HL	C	E	S	Pr	L
Fossil fuels	1 ✗	2 ✓	3	–	–	4	–	–
Geothermal power	–	–	–	–	–	–	–	5
Hydro-power	6	–	–	–	–	–	–	7
Wind power	8	9	–	–	10	–	–	11
Wave power	–	12	13	–	–	–	14	15
Solar power	16	17	18	19	–	–	–	20
Nuclear power	–	–	–	–	21	22	–	–

Key
R = Renewable
Pol = Polluting
HL = Add to earth's heat load
C = Cheap
E = Efficient
S = Safe
Pr = Practicable
L = Limited to certain areas

MARKING SCHEME

Your name _____

Grammar				Vocabulary				Reading		
	Total Score	Your Score			Total Score	Your Score			Total Score	Your Score
TEST 1										
Question 1 (Rec)	10	☐		Question 3	5	☐		Question 5	10	☐
Question 2 (Prod)	10	☐		Question 4	5	☐		Question 6	10	☐
Total	20	☐		Total	10	☐		Total	20	☐
TEST 2										
Question 1 (Rec)	10	☐		Question 4	5	☐		Question 6	5	☐
Question 2 (Prod)	5	☐		Question 5	5	☐		Question 7	5	☐
Question 3 (Prod)	5	☐						Question 8	10	☐
Total	20	☐		Total	10	☐		Total	20	☐
TEST 3										
Question 1 (Rec)	10	☐		Question 4	10	☐		Question 5	10	☐
Question 2 (Prod)	5	☐						Question 6	10	☐
Question 3 (Prod)	5	☐								
Total	20	☐		Total	10	☐		Total	20	☐
TEST 4										
Question 1 (Rec)	10	☐		Question 4	10	☐		Question 5	5	☐
Question 2 (Prod)	5	☐						Question 6	10	☐
Question 3 (Prod)	5	☐						Question 7	5	☐
Total	20	☐		Total	10	☐		Total	20	☐
TEST 5										
Question 1 (Rec)	10	☐		Question 3	10	☐		Question 4	10	☐
Question 2 (Prod)	10	☐						Question 5	10	☐
Total	20	☐		Total	10	☐		Total	20	☐

Grammar			Vocabulary			Reading		
TEST 6								
Question 1 (Rec)	10	☐	Question 3	10	☐	Question 4	6	☐
Question 2 (Prod)	10	☐				Question 5	8	☐
						Question 6	6	☐
Total	20	☐	Total	10	☐	Total	20	☐
TEST 7								
Question 1 (Rec)	10	☐	Question 3	10	☐	Question 4	8	☐
Question 2 (Prod)	10	☐				Question 5	12	☐
Total	20	☐	Total	10	☐	Total	20	☐
TEST 8								
Question 1 (Rec)	10	☐	Question 3	5	☐	Question 5	5	☐
Question 2 (Prod)	10	☐	Question 4	5	☐	Question 6	5	☐
						Question 7	10	☐
Total	20	☐	Total	10	☐	Total	20	☐
TEST 9								
Question 1 (Rec)	10	☐	Question 3	10	☐	Question 4	10	☐
Question 2 (Prod)	10	☐				Question 5	10	☐
Total	20	☐	Total	10	☐	Total	20	☐
TEST 10								
Question 1 (Rec)	10	☐	Question 3	10	☐	Question 4	10	☐
Question 2 (Prod)	10	☐				Question 5	10	☐
Total	20	☐	Total	10	☐	Total	20	☐
TEST 11								
Question 1 (Rec)	10	☐	Question 3	5	☐	Question 5	10	☐
Question 2 (Prod)	10	☐	Question 4	5	☐	Question 6	5	☐
						Question 7	5	☐
Total	20	☐	Total	10	☐	Total	20	☐

Grammar			Vocabulary			Reading		
TEST 12								
Question 1 (Rec)	10	☐	Question 3	5	☐	Question 5	10	☐
Question 2 (Prod)	10	☐	Question 4	5	☐	Question 6	10	☐
Total	20	☐	Total	10	☐	Total	20	☐
TEST 13								
Question 1 (Rec)	10	☐	Question 3	5	☐	Question 5	10	☐
Question 2 (Prod)	10	☐	Question 4	5	☐	Question 6	10	☐
Total	20	☐	Total	10	☐	Total	20	☐
TEST 14								
Question 1 (Rec)	10	☐	Question 3	10	☐	Question 4	10	☐
Question 2 (Prod)	10	☐				Question 5	10	☐
Total	20	☐	Total	10	☐	Total	20	☐
TEST 15								
Question 1 (Rec)	10	☐	Question 3	10	☐	Question 4	10	☐
Question 2 (Prod)	10	☐				Question 5	10	☐
Total	20	☐	Total	10	☐	Total	20	☐
TEST 16								
Question 1 (Rec)	10	☐	Question 3	5	☐	Question 5	10	☐
Question 2 (Prod)	10	☐	Question 4	5	☐	Question 6	10	☐
Total	20	☐	Total	10	☐	Total	20	☐